SHINE

DIGITAL CRAFTSMANSHIP
FOR MODERN LUXURY BRANDS

FLORINE EPPE BEAULOYE

What Others Are Saying

'If the social media revolution for brands was referred to as Branding 2.0, the *Shine* framework presented in this book should be referred to as Branding 3.0. Rare are the books that connect theory and practice in the way it is presented in *Shine – Digital Craftsmanship for Modern Luxury Brands*. You will appreciate the practical insights and how-to examples in the context of Luxury brands as well as the theory and principles which can be applied beyond the luxury brands' world. This book is certainly the one-stop-shop for anyone looking to learn how to make their brand *Shine* in the digital world of today.'

Fouad Howayek, Media Sales Manager, Asia Pacific, Facebook

'Digital Marketing Executives and CMOs will find this book helpful in shaping their thinking and their companies' digital strategies. Presenting a tried and trusted framework, Florine provides a structured discussion for developing a digital plan many luxury brands and companies can have in this highly connected world. If you are looking to connect more deeply with your consumers to gain better insights and to tell a more compelling story, you shall find this book stimulating.'

Jason Le, Team Lead, Google

'This book provides a fascinating look into a truly fascinating area— the mysterious world of luxury brands. The ideas in this book have been used by some of the most famous luxury brands in the world, in some of the world's most talked about campaigns. They've also been used to build small businesses with no budgets, to grow non-profit organisations—and even to help elect a president! I could not think of anyone better placed to help you navigate this area than Florine. Prepare to be taken from, as Florine puts it, 'OOPS' (Overwhelming Online Presence and Stress) to 'WOW' (Wonderful Online Wonderland)!'

Keith Browning, Marketing Manager, LinkedIn

'An absolutely well written book explaining the critical concepts of how a company should go digital in today's era. An easy and enjoyable read for anyone looking to grow their online presence.'

Vanessa Hemavathi, Program Director, Henley Business School (Executive Hedge Fund Program), Former Manager at *The Wall Street Journal*

'*Shine* is the digital marketing manual this segment badly needed. Unlike other business books, *Shine* isn't just theory—it's packed with practical examples and the questions your teams need to be asking to deliver luxury experiences in this digital era.'

Tobin Page, Chief Operating Officer, Publift

'Florine has delivered a timely piece which not only makes the utterly compelling case for luxury brands to fully embrace digital, but also lays out numerous real-world strategies to execute upon. Such a book is perfect in the hands of a CMO in need of clarity, and practitioners who wish to hone their skills. I'm grateful to have my own ideas shaken up thanks to Florine's insights.'

Keith Mander, Digital Entrepreneur

'As a luxury marketer, it is not always easy to embrace digital, and it can sometimes get overwhelming. Florine simplifies the digital concept, puts things in perspective and gives it suitable context, all the while providing examples, strategies, and practical recommendations based on her rich, professional knowledge. Her book leads readers through the vast digital landscape, helping them navigate its unfamiliar terrain, and ponder over relevant questions regarding its application to their businesses. I believe that *Shine* is a valuable tool for both CEOs and marketers, helping them understand the luxury market, and offering practical, yet remarkable insights and guidelines into how you can stay ahead through digital marketing.'

Justine Lacaille, Luxury Brand Manager

'Florine's book is a practical guide on how a luxury brand can be successful in the digital space. By clearly articulating why a brand should be online, she is helping the brand build a clear rationale as to why they should not overlook or underinvest in this space. Once a brand knows the 'Why', she then sets out to explain the 'How' in an easy-to-understand, yet comprehensive way, as she guides them on a journey from building their plan to measuring the results of their efforts. All of this is backed by real-world experience from her working with brands to help them establish a firm foothold in the digital world. A must-read for any luxury brand hoping to be successful online.'

Joe McDermottroe, Head of International Operations (Technology Entertainment), Former Manager at YouTube

Dedication

To my newborn son, William—you have changed my life in amazing ways. You won't remember me holding you in one arm as I typed my concluding notes with the other, but, I hope, someday, this book reminds you that you are an infinite source of happiness, inspiration and pride;

To my loving husband, Simon—you are my rock. Spending my life by your side is nothing short of extraordinary;

To my inspiring late father—your words of wisdom are a constant reminder to 'shine';

To you, the reader, and to all the resilient people of the world who are disrupting the status quo—it is my hope that this book might be your first step in elevating your brand and transforming people's lives... at scale.

Acknowledgements

Special thanks to…

My clients and partners who have graciously consented to sharing their stories,

All the luxury professionals who have shared their insights and expertise,

All the early readers for their reviews and endorsements,

My family for their endless and unconditional love, support and encouragement,

My better half, Simon, who was there to read my drafts, ask questions, and lend a comforting ear whenever I felt stuck, and for always believing in me,

My team and board of advisors at mOOnshot digital, my editors, my publisher,

…and all the people that have made this book possible.

Merci.

The Author

Florine Eppe Beauloye is an award-winning business strategist and luxury marketer with strong international experience spanning over a decade.

She is the Founder and CEO of mOOnshot digital (moonshotdigital. com), a pioneer boutique creative and digital marketing agency specialised in premium and luxury brands.

mOOnshot digital advises and collaborates with renowned luxury companies as well as emerging luxury brands worldwide.

Passionate about digital alchemy and a firm believer in the immeasurable value of the human touch in digital transformation, Florine specialises in shaping and polishing select brands and making them shine online, grow and capture hearts and minds.

A diverse yet coherent professional path has flown her across the world and given her a unique perspective on business and life. Her professional experience lies in discovering what is noteworthy, crafting compelling experiences and growing businesses.

She brings with her a broad perspective, having worked client side to drive business transformation from within award-winning businesses and as a Consultant across Europe and Asia, working across sectors such as Beauty & Wellness, Fashion, F&B, Retail E-Commerce,

Luxury Travel and Hospitality, covering all aspects of traditional and digital marketing and international communications.

Awarded one of the top 50 Asia's Woman Leaders by CMO Asia and World Brand Congress 2016, Florine is highly sought after for her opinions and insights on luxury marketing and digital transformation. She is also a regular guest speaker at universities, seminars, panel discussions and international conferences.

Florine holds a Master's degree in Marketing and Communication with First Class Honours from the Université libre de Bruxelles (ULB), a leading University in Belgium, Europe.

First published in Singapore 2017

Book production by Michael Hanrahan Publishing

ISBN: 978-0-9953900-0-3

Text design by Michael Hanrahan Publishing
Cover design by Peter Reardon
Creative direction by mOOnshot digital
Printed in Singapore by First Printers Pte Ltd

Contents

Foreword

As the CEO of The Luxury Network Singapore, I work very closely and regularly with key decision makers of premium and luxury brands.

It is in this context that I first met Florine Eppe Beauloye, Founder and CEO of mOOnshot digital, a pioneer boutique digital agency crafting bespoke digital solutions for premium and luxury brands. Florine is hardworking, diligent and passionate about digital marketing for luxury brands, and I am immensely pleased to be working closely with her.

In addition to her being a current member of The Luxury Network Singapore, mOOnshot digital is also our strategic digital partner. Florine and her team enlighten and advise us regarding our digital marketing strategies while we provide luxury expert opinions and insights.

Our strategic partnership also seeks to create new avenues of growth for luxury brands and high-end businesses by offering our elite members complete and tailored, online and offline marketing solutions. As Asia's luxury expert, we provide offline engagement opportunities such as targeted networking with luxury brands. Florine is a digital marketing expert specialised in fueling high-end brands with digital competence; she empowers these opportunities with her in-depth knowledge and experience in this arena.

Digital marketing has become a strategic component of luxury brands' business growth. Asia, in particular, has now entered the era of the informed consumer. The disposable income and level of education of luxury consumers have increased. They are now more empowered and connected. More people now own smartphones and have access to the internet than ever before.

The question is no longer if and when luxury brands should embrace the digital opportunity, but how they should go about doing it.

Digital is not just about having a social media account (such as LinkedIn, Facebook, Instagram, Twitter, etc.) and diligently posting information about your luxury brand. It is a lot more than that, and Florine's book *Shine – Digital Craftsmanship for Modern Luxury Brands* will enlighten you on these aspects.

Florine has the rare gift of making complex concepts accessible to her audiences. The book provides a much needed overview of the digital opportunities for the current luxury industry, and shares a simple framework to help answer the challenges of modern luxury management.

I would urge you to really engage with the book, which is powerful yet very accessible, and take the time to reflect at the end of each chapter and apply its principles.

The luxury sector is changing. Earlier, luxury brands referred solely to the traditional and well-known luxury brands. Not anymore. We now see the emergence of smaller, new aspirational brands. There is a higher demand for bespoke products and services, discreteness and cultural heritage. Consumers have become more sophisticated and their attitudes and preferences have changed. The definition of luxury is also different for different people. To some, luxury is something that is bespoke, while for others it could be something that is not available to the mass market.

One thing is certain: The only way for a luxury brand to stand out from the rest is by staying true to its DNA. This can be done through identifying one's DNA and properly communicating this, both offline and online, to its targeted audience. Florine's book offers a roadmap and recommendations on how this may be done.

This current and insightful book is an indispensable guide to those looking to understand the modern luxury industry and unlock the massive potential of digital as an invaluable means of enhancing the luxury experience and the sustainability of the luxury business.

I hope after you have read this book you will be convinced to strengthen your luxury digital experience.

Irene Ho
CEO, The Luxury Network Singapore

Embracing Change

It is not the strongest of the species
that survive, nor the most intelligent, but
the ones most responsive to change.

—LEON C. MEGGINSON, REFERRING TO THE WORK OF CHARLES DARWIN

CHARLES Darwin may not have been a marketer by trade, but his theories reflect today's reality more than ever before. Think about it: change is inevitable. How we work, entertain, communicate and live are constantly changing and new technologies are taking centre stage. The world is going through a digital transformation as everything—and everyone—becomes more connected and interconnected.

New technologies are fuelling disruptive innovations and forever changing the business landscape. Innovators are moving boundaries and questioning the status quo at an unprecedented pace.

In 1994, Amazon.com was launched and revolutionised the way we buy books. Today e-commerce and online shopping are becoming mainstream.

In 1998, Google made the whole web searchable. Today it's hard to imagine business (and even life) without Google there to answer our every question and need in a matter of seconds. In fact, Google is now such an integral part of our lives that its brand name has officially become a verb in the Oxford English Dictionary. People don't 'search for something online', they 'Google it'.

Google has become the 'business card' of reference for businesses around the world and is so influential that if people cannot find your business high up on Google's search results, they simply assume it does not exist or at least is not worthy.

In 2004, social media was born and changed forever the way we communicate with relatives and friends, like-minded strangers, partners and brands around the globe. Word-of-mouth now has the power to travel fast, and far. People want to contribute to unscripted discussions, share their life experiences and be heard. We look for instant responses and gratification. We expect real-time interactions. We value unique experiences over product features.

Launched in 2005, YouTube has now revolutionised the way we consume videos and share original content. Today, 300 hours of footage is uploaded to YouTube every single minute! YouTube also launched careers and revealed emerging artists to the world—whether we like him or not, Justin Bieber is a great example of the power of YouTube. This (then unknown) teenage singer got his start by uploading his recordings that then went viral, soon attracting the attention of Usher's label, which decided to sign him.

'YouTube famous' is now part of our cultural lexicon in reference to those individuals with a huge YouTube fan base. These digital influencers can be more famous than mainstream celebrities, especially among millennials, and can reach massive audiences (sometimes with millions of subscribers) and engage with them on a whole new level. From beauty and fashion tips from Zoe Sugg (a.k.a. Zoella) to surprisingly hypnotic unboxing, such as the much-hyped tech gadgets reviews from Unbox Therapy—where they quite literally unpack a product to get a feel for it—these YouTube uploaders are having a huge influence on how we consume and engage with products.

LinkedIn is another digital disrupter, and I vividly remember when I first discovered the site. It was 2006, and I was in the very early stage of my career. A friend of mine sent me an invite to join the online business network, telling me it could help me connect with and reach potential employers through trusted referrals. LinkedIn was just over three years old at the time and, even though it already had 5 million users, it was not widely used among my professional network and friends. It sometimes even felt like a 'ghost town' with little social traction. But it was new. It was different. And it offered the chance for me to gain 'exclusive access' to senior professionals outside of my direct reach. So it was definitely exciting.

Less than a decade later and with over 414 million users, LinkedIn has become the business network of reference. People now check your LinkedIn profile and learn about your professional background before they meet you over coffee and look at your resume.

In 2007, Apple Inc. introduced the iPhone, and in so doing transformed the face of smartphones. Smartphones are now widespread across the globe, and increasingly blur the line between home and work—even more than laptops did before them. Some statistics even claim that more people own a mobile phone than a toothbrush.

The point is this. Digital is shortening innovation cycles and is a driving force for brands and people who know how to take advantage of the new digital media and technologies. For businesses, this new connected reality means having to take a holistic approach to digital and adopting a 'digital first' mindset to stay relevant.

Digital is here to stay and will continue to evolve. It will become faster, and stronger. Super-fast internet connection, mobile devices, cloud computing, wearables, and the number of social networks will all continue to proliferate. New technologies will continue to converge to answer consumer needs before we even crystallise these needs in our own minds.

So to grow your business and stay relevant in this new context, you will have to shake things up, do things differently, adopt the right digital mindset and adapt quickly.

You are at a crossroad. You have an important choice to make right now, right here. You have only two ways to regard change in your business and your choice is going to determine the relevance and success of your business in the months and years to come. You can choose to adapt, to lean in and to win. Or you can resist change and watch your business slowly fade away.

Luxury Marketing: Adding a Touch of Class

Whether through fear or conservative thinking, luxury brands have generally been slower to embrace digital. Instead, they have tended to look at the rise of digital innovation from a distance, remaining sceptical. Many have seemed overwhelmed by the complexity, and the perceived threat to exclusivity and other aspects of traditional luxury posed by the ubiquity of digital. Even among those luxury marketers who now understand they need to embrace digital, many still seem confused about where to start.

Traditionally, the luxury sector has relied heavily on traditional marketing strategies with tightly controlled and carefully crafted one-way communications—the brand's story captured through glossy print advertising, for example, or TV commercials endorsed by celebrity brand ambassadors. Luxury brands have also relied on face-to-face interactions, invitation-only events, and that personalised attention and impeccable 'white-glove' in-store service they pride themselves on providing—for example, the sales associate who, just like your personal shopper, remembers your last purchase and can now suggest another item to complement your outfit and style.

These traditional strategies have served luxury brands well, and they don't need to be discarded in this digital age. Adopting new cutting-edge technologies does not mean forgetting your brand's history or heritage or even diluting your luxury values. Instead, having to deal with the increasing power of digital and mobile means understanding new tools and platforms, new processes, and, most importantly, new relationships and changed consumer behaviours.

So although digital can be overwhelming and frightening, especially for high-end brands, the promise and potential it holds is far greater than you imagine. With digital entrenched in our daily lives, the convergence of luxury and digital is here to stay. Digital marketing is really only in its infancy, and there are still so many opportunities to be uncovered.

Your consumers no longer blindly trust carefully crafted, one-way commercial messages. Brands are expected to engage customers with truthful, emotional and meaningful stories, and to communicate these stories through multiple channels. They are also expected to encourage their customers to contribute to these stories and their experience of the brand. Because let's face it, people can now access the finest things in life and discover new emerging brands at the click of a button, anytime, anywhere.

DIGITAL SPARKLE

The message for luxury brands is loud and clear: to stay relevant you must lean in and transform from a brand-centric and traditional model to a fully integrated and more customer-centric organisation.

Throughout this book, I include examples of luxury brands that are winning in digital narratives. Importantly, through the following chapters I also provide strategies and tips to help you future-proof your business. I equip you with a framework to help you build an overarching strategy and jumpstart your organisation's digital journey. And I share plenty of insights and practical recommendations to help you grow.

You are reading this book, so congratulations! This is your first step towards digital enlightenment.

A Book Filled with Little Luxuries

Although some luxury brands have started to move forward and embrace digital, a wide gap still exists between most brands' current strategies and how luxury brands should behave online. Crafting compelling digital experiences for your luxury brand, however, requires a deep understanding of how luxury shoppers use digital— and that is where this book comes in.

Digital is about much more than just the technology. Digital is, above all, about people and the opportunity to truly, deeply connect with your audience and radically transform people's lives at scale.

The new reality is that digital marketing and traditional marketing should no longer be managed in isolation. Instead, you need to be looking at integrated marketing strategies for the digital age. These strategies are about leveraging new tools and new technologies, combined with the best storytelling magic from traditional marketing, to engage with modern and discerning customers.

These concepts apply equally to all luxury brands, regardless of their size, and when I decided to write this book on the exciting topic of digital marketing for premium and luxury brands, I decided I also wanted to focus on helping SME and niche luxury businesses, in particular, grow and sustain in this digital age. Large international brands often get all the attention when discussing the luxury sector. So in this book I've focused on providing the key drivers of success and the strategies for growth that can be implemented by the numerous premium SMEs and niche luxury brands—all the amazing brands that provide master artisanal craftsmanship and have outstanding products or services but somehow get lost and remain unnoticed because they do not know how to leverage digital effectively. And that's why this book contains some little luxuries as well—examples from smaller and niche luxury brands that I've worked with or that I feel are innovators in the digital space.

Even before I started working with luxury brands, I'd already developed a sense for beautiful design, a passion for excellence and an uncompromising attitude towards quality—indeed, this is perhaps why I enjoy so much working with luxury brands today. (While some of my classmates were considered 'cool kids', I was known to be the 'perfectionist', scoring a mark of 11 out of 10 for a design project because the teacher felt I had exceeded even the full mark expectations.)

My first purchasing experience with a 'true' luxury piece from a global luxury brand was in 2002, when I bought a Louis Vuitton wallet. Even today, this wallet continues to awaken the memories of that very special moment and all the adventures I had while I was living and working in Dublin, Ireland. The art of stylish travel and the concept of the metaphorical journey of life are fundamentally encapsulated in Louis Vuitton's heritage, and these values resonate with me as a global nomad at heart. These very personal perceptions and associated connections are exactly what luxury is all about, and it's this emotional value that really makes a luxury brand what it is.

Throughout this book, I offer ways to build distinctive brand experiences that evoke those powerful emotional bonds.

As you may already be aware, digital marketing is in constant evolution and requires continuous learning, and I do not profess to be an absolute authority on the luxury industry or digital marketing. But in the course of my work with some fascinating luxury brands and premium SMEs across Europe and Asia, I have had the privilege of working alongside many business owners, CEOs and marketing managers, gathering valuable insights and accompanying them on their journey of digital relevance. I want to share all these stories and more with you.

As a marketing strategist and consultant, I have been passionately following the exciting evolution of digital and its implications for premium and luxury brands. I have seen many wonderful brands, established and emerging, struggle with the same issues and challenges. The most resounding of these were linked to how to effectively leverage digital to successfully establish their luxurious brand in this market, with maximum return on investment and without sacrificing their premium or luxury brand's values and innate exclusive positioning. I have experienced firsthand the difficulties for premium and luxury SMEs and niche brands in navigating through the unfamiliar digital sea without being wiped out by the powerful waves that keep coming back ... and back, stronger. I have witnessed a huge shift in the way we do marketing and seen so many brands waste money, time and energy, and miss opportunities either by ignorance or misaligned strategies. Understanding those challenges provides invaluable lessons, and learning to overcome them is part and parcel of growing a successful business.

Having worked both in-house and on the agency side, I've gained a holistic understanding of the full marketing ecosystem. I've also been able to develop some powerful frameworks and strategies that can be adapted by all luxury brands, no matter their size or target market. These frameworks include my *Shine* model, which can help you develop a flexible and individual approach for your digital strategy. I have outlined this in more detail in chapter 5.

This book is written to help *you*, whether you are a forward-thinking CEO, the owner of a premium SME, a luxury marketer, or a budding entrepreneur who understands the need to go digital but does not know how to do it right. Or perhaps you're a business and marketing student who will soon enter the workforce to start your career in a premium SME or in the luxury sector. This book is also for you. Although dedicated to premium and luxury brands, virtually any business can benefit from applying some of the digital principles contained in this book to increase their brand's online desirability and offer a more polished and first-class user experience.

In the following pages, I examine the common struggles and winning strategies of premium and luxury brands. I have deliberately chosen to highlight both the good and not so good in various case studies to paint a realistic picture and so help you better appreciate what the digital journey entails and avoid common pitfalls.

This book is divided into two main parts: 'The Why' and 'The How'. Part 1, 'The Why', sets out the rationale behind the importance of digital for the luxury sector and explains the new and uncertain territory in which luxury now finds itself. In part 2, 'The How', I provide insights, strategies and a simple framework that you can use to move your business forward.

This book is about demystifying digital marketing and equipping you with both insights and practical advice. I do not want to confuse you with heaps of marketing buzzwords and clichéd digital tactics. Instead, I have kept the jargon to a minimum and focused on ensuring that the information and analyses provided in this book are as relatable and timeless as possible, so that they may be applied to your own context, wherever and whenever. The simple but effective framework provided in this book will help you realise your full potential through digital innovation. I have included some 'digital sparkle' through the chapters, to highlight important insights or tips, and have added questions at the end of every chapter to help you reflect and ponder on what you have read. Asking yourself these questions can help you see more clearly how digital can shape and grow your business into a stronger brand.

Be warned: the path will be bumpy at times. This book will also challenge you. After all, magic is known to happen beyond your comfort zone, and innovation always starts with a 'can-do' attitude and, most importantly, the willingness to create value—value for your customers and for your business (in this particular order).

This is not a technical book and nor is it about providing one magic formula for digital success. What worked yesterday may not bring you success tomorrow. To see future opportunities, you will need to let go of some of your old and traditional marketing thinking, challenge accepted norms, and be open to learning new concepts, and experiment. I hope this book's recommendations and insights will lead you through the right digital mindset to grow your premium or luxury brand and achieve sustainable brand value in the digital age. It's all about planting the seeds so you can harvest the fruits for months and years to come.

In essence, in this competitive and highly connected world, only the most forward-thinking and ambitious brands will become enduring brand champions. This will only happen with practice, persistence and discipline, with the support of their loving fans and supporters, and with the execution and drive to win.

My goal is simple: to help you move from what I call an 'OOPS' (Overwhelming Online Presence and Stress) situation to a 'WOW' (Wonderful Online Wonderland) state. I hope you find some value in this book and that it starts you on the path to WOW, and to becoming a successful, digitally empowered business.

If you are ready, let's begin your digital journey.

PART 1

THE WHY

In this age of the customer, the
only sustainable competitive advantage
is knowledge of and engagement
with customers.

—DAVID M. COOPERSTEIN, FORRESTER RESEARCH

CHAPTER 1

A New Definition of Luxury

LUXURY. A word that used to connote privileged indulgence and rank. But digitisation combined with globalisation and a shift in earning power have fuelled new expectations for luxury. So what does luxury really mean today? Is the traditional definition still relevant in the digital age?

Before we look at the modern definition of luxury, let's look backwards at the origin of the term. Derived from the Latin word 'luxuria', which relates to excess, 'luxury' historically revolved around its inherent opulence, comfort or elegance, steeped in its connections to royals, nobles and aristocrats. Luxury was the privilege of the rich and famous, involving great expense, and was meant to express refined taste and impress crowds. It was exclusively enjoyed by the elite and unattainable to the 'masses'.

In *The Road To Luxury* (2015), Ashok Som and Christian Blanckaert define luxury brands as those that have been carefully crafted through meticulous strategies in marketing and brand building, embedding themselves in the consumer's subconscious and having the following main characteristics: brand strength, differentiation, exclusivity, innovation, product craftsmanship and precision, premium pricing, and high quality.

In our modern society, the term 'luxury' is becoming harder to define, but as highlighted by Luxury Daily, some time-proven qualities haven't changed: luxury still involves exceptional craftsmanship and customer service, brand authenticity, limited distribution and high perceived value.

In this chapter, I explore what luxury means to modern consumers and how these perceptions can affect luxury brands—especially SMEs and niche brands.

Beyond Bling

Luxury has become younger. Once largely confined to an older, more conservative clientele, younger generations are now moving into the luxury market, and disrupting it their way. According to James B.

Twitchell, in his 2002 book *Living It Up: America's Love Affair with Luxury*, affluent consumers are now 'younger than clients of the old luxury used to be, they are far more numerous, they make their money far sooner, and they are far more flexible in financing and fickle in choice'.

But as much as luxury is changing, it is also remaining the same.

DIGITAL SPARKLE

Luxury is now both timeless and current—timeless because it is full of history and leaves a lasting, indelible impression, and current because it needs to answer to modern affluent consumers.

The connection between luxury and quality is also unchanged. Luxury never, ever, negotiates on quality, and excellence is at the core. This excellence is earned and consistently delivered.

So what does this tell you? Luxury remains an emotional purchase, and the quest for personal satisfaction is still intrinsic to any luxury product or service. Luxury has been, and will always be, about how it makes us feel.

The objective of this book is not about searching for the most accurate definition of luxury, though. Instead, it's about understanding how consumers are shaping luxury brands today and how these exclusive brands can leverage digital.

The modern context seems to be shifting from simply acquiring high-end products per se to being more about acquiring first-class, authentic, one-of-a-kind experiences. It's now more than ever about *experiencing* luxury rather than owning it. This is not to say that the desire for luxury goods has been completely replaced with the desire for lavish experiences, but the latter is certainly growing strongly. The 13th edition of the *Bain Luxury Study*, published by Bain & Company, for example, reported that international travel and tourism is fuelling an appetite for 360-degree luxury experiences, such as high-end transportation that includes highly customised supercars and yachts, as well as luxury hotels and cruises.

If luxury used to be mainly marketed via tangible objects and is now moving more towards experiences, what has always really made a brand a luxury one are the intangibles: heritage, craftsmanship, savoir faire, myth. And to capitalise on this, all luxury brands have to tell stories. This has always been the case, but it is now especially important in the digital age. We will explore this point in greater detail in later chapters in this book.

Entering the New World of Luxury

Luxury has traditionally been seen as desired by many, but owned by few. Today, however, the world of luxury is evolving to target a wider audience, and the boundaries of luxury have extended to the aspiring middle class. In Singapore and other parts of Asia (where the growth of this luxury market is most notable) luxury has become a seeming necessity—as manifested by the queues in front of Louis Vuitton and other luxury brands' flagship stores. We have also witnessed a certain form of democratisation of the desire of luxury—which does not translate through to lower pricing but to a wider audience interested in luxury products.

Another consideration when discussing modern luxury is that perceptions may vary according to countries. For example, Coach New York is perceived as a premium brand in Europe while it is positioned as a luxury brand in Asia.

With the emergence of a mass class of wealthy people, 'indulging' in occasional luxury has become more common. Luxury is in this case considered a treat, not a lifestyle. People want, for example, to have a once-in-a-lifetime 'experience' honeymoon, or splurge on an unbelievable weekend in one of the best hotels in the world. Or they may indulge in that rare luxury item to work in with their other, more mainstream, items.

We indulge in everyday luxuries, bite-sized luxuries, affordable luxuries or occasional luxuries—whatever you prefer to call it. Whether it be a pair of red-soled Christian Louboutin stilettos, designer clothes, a pampering day at a luxurious spa, the luxurious feel of a rich chocolate macaron from Maison Ladurée, the latest high-tech gadget, a romantic dinner at a Michelin-starred restaurant or an elevated evening with a Glenmorangie Single Malt, we all like to find some way to access modern luxuries. How often we are able to indulge may vary significantly, but the desire to indulge now exists for a much wider, more nuanced market.

Of course, my perception of luxury may differ from yours, and has changed through my life. From a modest family, I certainly didn't inherit a lifelong membership to 'high society'. I was born in a remote town in the Democratic Republic of the Congo (then known as Zaire), Africa—a town that was so remote, its name, Mbanza-Ngungu, is unknown to most and difficult to pronounce for all.

I had never really paid any attention to 'branded' things until the middle of secondary school, when I noticed that most of my classmates had a Kipling (a premium fashion brand from Belgium) while I carried a non-branded school bag. I also remember running on the athletic tracks with my unbranded sport outfits and shoes, while other kids were sporting obvious brands. So my first pair of Nike running spikes were, for me, a luxury. The first time I enjoyed an exquisite scoop of Haagen Dazs' cookies and cream ice cream during my university years was, again, luxury to me. My weekend in a comfortable hotel in the Whitsundays Islands after almost a year on the road backpacking around Australia—also luxury to me.

Coming from this background, I distinctly remember the very first time I flew business class with Etihad Airways. Having travelled to 31 countries and 238 cities, I had been flying in economy class for years but business class was a revelation. And it wasn't just the extra legroom and being able to have a proper sleep that drew me in. It was the pleasure of skipping the long queue at check-in. It was the opportunity to relax in the lounge while waiting for the flight to board, along with the chance to freshen up and enjoy a complimentary spa treatment in Abu Dhabi before arriving at my final destination. It was the quality of the food served, and the special attention of the aircraft crew who knew me by name. The overall experience was the real value for me.

As I grew up and earned more spending power, I started to genuinely appreciate luxury goods for their remarkable quality and craftsmanship, and admire them for their sleek and stylish design. I was attracted by their stories and the aura that surrounds them and makes them so desirable. To me, luxury isn't about buying expensive things and nor is it superficial; it is about the desire to experience memorable and meaningful moments. I love the thought of being part of that dream. So I started indulging in occasional luxury goods and luxurious experiences to celebrate some of my key life milestones—a lavish yet intimate tropical wedding in Bali, for example, and an exquisite honeymoon in the Maldives and remote parts of Namibia. I also love the experiences I've had access to that money can't buy, such as an exclusive invite to Le Festival de Cannes red carpet event among Hollywood celebrities.

My point is this. Luxury means different things to different people and generations. Essentially, luxury is in the eye of the beholder and changes over time. Luxury is very much defined by your maturity and purchasing power.

The expression of luxury, in its new context, has become more subtle and understated, more personal, individualistic and intimate, and less ostentatious. You have most likely noticed how luxury brands have progressively toned down their 'logo-covered' products. Luxury is now all about offering consumers something outside of their ordinary experiences, with consumers wanting to bring their own personality to the products and experiences they purchase, and for these products and experiences to be an expression of their own personal creativity. Luxury is now about inclusivity and this authentic connection between brand values and the consumers' own personal stories. Consumers often don't want to take one complete 'look' straight off the catwalk, for example. They want more fluidity than that, and to be able to inject what they buy with their own meaning, and their own twist.

More and more, affluent consumers are combining the high with the low. This is where you see fashionistas wearing H&M or Zara clothing while holding a Louis Vuitton or Prada bag. In addition, we have seen more high-profile collaborations happening between luxury labels and mass retailers to offer mainstream capsule collections, with examples including Stella McCartney for Adidas, or Alexander Wang and Balmain for H&M.

As our attitudes towards luxury evolve, a growing trend towards 'experiential marketing' is emerging. Experiential marketing hooks into this need for meaning and is all about amplifying the essence of a luxury product with interactive and memorable experiences that reinforce its stature. This trend is all about recognising consumers as emotional beings, aspiring to achieve pleasurable experiences and lifestyles. As mentioned, the growth of certain luxury categories such as quality alcohol, fine food and bespoke travel signal that consumer values are transitioning from pure materialism towards 'one-of-a-kind' experiences, from extrinsic to intrinsic and from conspicuous to authentic, meaningful and personalised.

Creating immersive brand experiences has thus become a key focus for luxury brands. Think about all the little things that leave a memorable impression—from high-touch service to unique packaging and interactive environments that create or enhance the synergy between the brand and the affluent consumer.

I am a big fan of travel and have had the chance to experience some unique and amazing places the world over. When it comes to high-touch service, one property in particular always comes to mind: Alila Villas Uluwatu. Sitting on the edge of a limestone cliff, offering panoramic views of the Indian Ocean, this boutique resort in Bali is a great example of personalised luxury experience done well.

My husband and I stayed in one of their one-bedroom villas in 2013 and we can still vividly recall their attention to detail and personalised touch. Upon booking, we were emailed a link to a sleek landing page asking us to answer some questions about our personal preferences—including our desired type of pillow, our ideal room temperature, our relaxing music of choice, our preferred level of service (from private, a-la-demande butler service to indulgent, full-time dedicated butler). The moment we entered the property and were greeted, we felt we were staying somewhere special. Upon check-in, everything was according to our taste. Then, throughout our stay, the staff never failed to surprise us with small attentions—including attaching a personalised luggage tag with our names on our suitcases before sending them to our room. Now that's what I call bespoke luxury hospitality. What made it so memorable for my husband and me was the attention to detail, and the care shown to us.

When thinking of this experiential approach, think of the Burberry flagship store in London that showcases relevant catwalk and other filmed content on nearby screens to engage consumers and immerse them in the 'Burberry experience'. Think of how Hermès took a selection of its craftsmen on tour to major cities as part of its Festival des Métiers program to showcase their work and demonstrate the expertise involved in creating their high-end products. These are brand journeys to be experienced and shared.

Affluent consumers want to be invited to exclusive previews, and to gain privileged access to what happens behind the scenes. My agency, mOOnshot digital, is the exclusive digital agency for The Luxury Network Singapore, a private business-to-business club for premier brands and organisations. As a luxury member, I am regularly invited to exclusive events for some of the world's most renowned luxury brands—such as an invitation to attend Tom Ford's runway collection and fragrance launch. And I can assure you that the brands that leave me with a memorable impression all benefit from it in the long run.

Globalisation and the internet also mean we are more aware of what exists outside of our immediate realm, and have more access to this 'insider knowledge' than ever before. Luxury is more accessible for more people—at least to virtually 'touch' it, to find out about its history and what it might be planning for the future, and to dream about it. We can compare. We can easily discover and gain access to aspirational brands. We can look for bespoke products or services. When your product is hand-made or customised, it is the ultimate luxury.

Perceptions of luxury are now more individual. What's luxury for you might not be for me. We are now in an era of individual empowerment. The focus for consumers—and for brands—is now on building people's individual uniqueness.

One of my clients, Uomo Group, is the exclusive distributor in Singapore of Brioni—the label that dressed some of the world's most elegant men, including James Bond (well, the actors who play James Bond in the movies). Upon entering their luxurious boutique in Marina Bay Sands (one of the most prestigious shopping mall destinations in Singapore), you will always receive an exclusive dressing experience. You are brought to a Personal Shopping Suite (within the VIP lounge) and served champagne or whisky as your sales associate takes your measurements and records your personal preferences. But what really defines Brioni is the personalised, *su misura* (meaning 'made to order' in Italian) service. Each suit takes between 18 and 22 hours to make, involves 220 individual steps, and contains between 7000 and 9000 stitches sewn by hand. When Brioni crafted my husband's wedding suit, we were able to decide on and choose every single detail—from the fabric to the shape and design of the buttons. The result of this freedom to choose, coupled with intricate craftsmanship, is a suit customised to each man's personality, and their ideal look and lifestyle.

As mentioned, besides the evolving definition and perceptions of what constitutes modern luxury, *who* has access to luxury is changing too, and I shall talk more about the new generation of tech-savvy luxury consumers in chapter 4.

Watching the Rise of Global Niche Luxury Brands

When you think of luxury, the ultimate global luxury giants likely to come to mind are Hermès, Prada, Tiffany & Co., Chanel, Louis Vuitton, Cartier, Rolex and many more. Many traditional luxury brands have their origins in Europe, a continent seen by many as the 'natural' home of high style and fine craftsmanship.

But nowadays, new concepts of luxury seem to be proliferating and adding nuance to the definition of traditional luxury. You may have heard of terms such as 'new luxury', 'masstige', 'ultra-premium' or 'affordable luxury'. Each of these terms is trying to identify a new niche or variance of luxury.

In this book, I go beyond the traditional luxury market, composed as it is of very exclusive and established brands with strong heritage. I believe there has never been a better time in history for luxury small businesses and niche brands to behave big. Digital avenues provide everyone new powers to innovate anywhere in the world. And the growing middle class has higher disposable incomes to spend on experiencing hedonic products, along with a desire to use luxury goods to express their creativity and uniqueness.

These factors combine to suggest that focusing on your niche market can be very powerful for your brand. Contrary to what many may think, by narrowing your niche you can actually widen your opportunity.

But before we look at the forces driving the emergence and success of niche brands, what is a niche brand?

A niche brand is a brand that is usually distributed on a smaller scale and is not as established as a mainstream brand. A niche brand will have one strong focal point and target a more narrowly defined subset of the market. Importantly, finding your niche is not just about finding a specialisation—it's also about finding the most profitable segment of your market. Many businesses are afraid to narrow down their target audience to a specific niche, afraid that it might reduce their revenue potential. But truth is, if you can define a great niche and know how to really connect with it, your business will thrive.

So why is this the case? Why are new luxury challengers coming out to play with the grown-up traditional power brands?

The internet has facilitated the development of niche luxury brands and made previously difficult-to-find brands accessible. And while digital has allowed smaller businesses to find a market globally, it has also allowed them to innovate and do almost everything a big company can do. Because of this, new, younger and more dynamic luxury brands are entering the market—brands that can rely heavily on digital to make a name. They no longer need a big marketing team or budget to reach the affluent consumers in today's market. Digital is addressing common pain points (such as within distribution networks, access to deep knowledge and resources, and transaction costs), and facilitating a smarter way for emerging brands to do business. Niche luxury brands can also scale much more quickly than traditional companies by opting for very lean and agile processes. This means that, if momentum builds behind a particular product, they can get more out to consumers without losing their luxury feel.

The younger generation, in particular, has more diversified tastes, is culturally curious, has nurtured a desire for product personalisation, and is much more demanding about what it is willing to purchase. Collectively, niche brands offer a wide range of choices for affluent consumers who increasingly seek novelty and want to express their individualism. These consumers are more individualised than ever, expecting every product, service and experience purchased to address their unique and highly personalised needs.

DIGITAL SPARKLE

Affluent consumers have countless choices, both online and in-store, so they're searching for something different, something that really grabs them and seems to speak directly to them.

These discerning consumers are also more knowledgeable and connected than ever before. They can compare. They can actively hunt for the best of the best. Just by browsing the internet, affluent consumers are increasingly able to learn about, compare and discover new brands and trends, and explore the next big emerging designers. Today's increasingly sophisticated consumers recognise innovation, quality and artisanal craftsmanship, and are always on the lookout for originality—and so are turning more and more to niche luxury brands.

Today's market is more segmented, and with this segmentation comes great opportunities for smaller and emerging brands. Niche luxury players are nibbling at the market share of more established brands, and this niche approach is particularly noticeable in the fragrance industry. From using fine quality (and often exotic and rare) ingredients to offering highly personalised service and well-trained frontline staff, niche perfumes answer the ever-increasing desire of discerning consumers for individualism—in this case, with unique, more differentiated and personalised scents. Relying less on celebrity marketing and focusing more on the originality of the scent, the quality of the ingredients and artistic integrity, niche perfume brands—such as pioneers L'Artisan Parfumeur (recently acquired by Puig), Jo Malone (now owned by Estée Lauder) and more recently Roja Parfums—have won the hearts of a growing number of consumers. Such scents allow our personality to shine through, connect us with powerful memories, and are silent extensions of our innermost desires.

A great example of a global niche luxury perfume house mastering the art of bespoke perfumery is Fragrance Du Bois (known as Parfums

Du Bois in France). Sustainably sourcing the finest raw materials from across the globe, Fragrance Du Bois has built its unique concept around its signature oud (or agarwood, a rare resinous heartwood derived from Aquilaria trees) oil-based fragrances.

Fragrance du Bois provides exclusive services, from semi-bespoke experiences (whereby customers can request adjustments to one of the existing perfumes) to true bespoke experiences (which involves the master perfumer creating a unique scent and bottle specifically based on your personality).

In the new digital landscape, SMEs and niche brands in particular will greatly benefit from occupying a brand space in the minds of consumers that is highly differentiated—or, better still, distinctive.

PAUSE AND PONDER

- What's your vision for what you hope to fulfil in the marketplace?

- Do you understand the value that your brand offers that truly differentiates you from your competitors?

- Have you determined what luxury means for your brand?

- Can you define your niche?

- Is your brand portraying a unique lifestyle?

CHAPTER 2

Digital and Luxury —the Alchemy of Paradoxes

THE digital revolution is happening. The impact of technology since the late twentieth century has been profound, but the digital transformation businesses are now primed to experience is much more disruptive. In this chapter, I take you through these changes, what they might mean for luxury brands, and how you can use them to your advantage.

The New Digital Game: Participate or Perish

You're likely already aware of the regrettable fate of photography giant Kodak. At its peak, Kodak was a trusted and leading brand worldwide—so much so that a Kodak camera and film were used on the Apollo 11 moon landing in 1969. But the brand was brought down by its own refusal to recognise the power of digital. Believe it or not, a Kodak engineer is credited with inventing the first digital camera in the mid 1970s, but the idea was not explored. If only Kodak had evolved its business model and recognised the opportunity—it could have led the digital revolution from the front. Instead, it failed to adapt to the digital transformation and filed for bankruptcy in 2012. Kodak was simply out-innovated by its competitors and succumbed to nimble newcomers.

All brands can learn two great lessons from this story:

- *Explore and experiment fast; refine later:* experiment with multiple approaches and ideas. More than ever before, businesses must be agile. Start with an idea, test it quickly, and progressively build on it. The biggest mistake made by many businesses is that they are so comfortable in their traditional space that they ignore the new realities until it is too late. I explore these ideas further throughout this book.
- *Change the culture within your organisation to successfully embrace change:* change must be adopted by your entire organisation in order to succeed.

These ideas of constant experimentation and change can seem like anathema to owners of traditional luxury brands, who may feel they have built their whole brand story around constancy and reliability. However, this book was born from the realisation that luxury brands—and in particular niche and less established brands—have a huge opportunity to thrive in this digital age, using digital to reinforce the integrity and bespoke craftsmanship behind the brand. Digital has levelled the playing field, so it is one that does not necessarily favour the big players over the smaller ones anymore. The problem is, luxury brands—big and small—often fail in the execution of their digital strategy.

Traditionally, marketing your business to make it stand out was always linked to a hefty budget. However, with the emergence of digital marketing, reaching out to the right audience and increasing your brand presence—and, ultimately, your revenue—is not only possible but has also become quite cost effective.

DIGITAL SPARKLE

It's no longer those who spend the most on marketing who necessarily get the best results. What does get results is based more on how much you connect with your audience and the value you are able to bring to them.

Today, a small business with a premium niche brand can succeed in global markets by adopting a proactive and agile approach to digital, and we're increasingly seeing emerging brands win over more established businesses through digital innovation.

When interviewing luxury professionals and researching for the book, I also realised something interesting. Most people tend to think that all luxury brands have big marketing budgets. But this is actually not always the case. Many premium and luxury niche brands (even those within an international luxury group) are managed like individual SMEs, with their own P&L, limitations and restrictions. Many international luxury brands also commonly rely on local premium distributors (in particular, across Asia and the Middle East) to manage their brands in those markets, acknowledging that they may not fully understand local cultures and retail specificities. For those local distributors, it can be difficult to promote those luxury brands because they are highly dependent on the principal's decisions regarding most marketing and communication initiatives. This results in marketing or branding campaigns that are slower to react and overall cautious—again creating opportunities that smaller, more nimble niche brands can exploit.

High Class and High Tech

As market needs and trends shift, luxury brands that do not embrace digital will be left on the sidelines. Digital is key to keeping your business relevant in the marketplace—it is so powerful, it actually has the power to make your business succeed or fail. Likely you already understand this. Digital has quickly evolved into a strategic priority for most businesses. However, if many businesses now understand that they need to embrace digital, often they don't truly understand what that *really* encompasses for their premium or luxury brands.

Put simply, digital is the broad range of technology-enabled advancements that are transforming how we live our lives and how businesses operate. Digital is the convergence of social media, mobile, the web, big data and cloud computing. But digital is a word with many meanings. If you ask what 'digital' actually means to a group of people, chances are every single response will be different. And it should be! But there is one shared reality: digital is a disruptive force and those who resist it will most certainly lose big time over the months and years to come.

Instead of looking at digital as a pure technical disrupter, however, businesses should concentrate on how to best cater for the behavioural changes that come with it. Digital is reshaping consumer behaviours, unlike anything we have seen before—think 24/7 connected consumers. These 'always on' luxury shoppers heavily rely on the internet for search and discovery. So digital is no longer a 'nice to have'. Digital is essential. The question whether 'to be, or not to be' online is no longer valid. The more complicated question you should be asking relates to how well you can play in this digital context and how you can provide your consumers with a new remarkable experience. But don't feel overwhelmed—I cover how to implement a winning digital strategy in part 2 of this book.

Digital opens the doors to amazing opportunities, and the innovative brands are those gaining the favour of customers. The desire for seamless, personalised experiences and rich, engaging content will only continue to grow. Luxury brands that don't keep pace with their customers' digital behaviours and preferences will fall behind, whereas those that bring the right experiences to their discerning customers at the right moment will outperform competitors. But luxury brands that provide frustrating and bad online experiences may actually damage their brands. The challenge for your luxury brand is that it is judged by slightly higher standards than more 'mass market' brands and businesses.

When building your luxury brand—telling its story, creating experiences for your customers—you have to learn to play by the new rules of digital engagement and go beyond some common misconceptions. Don't think the rules are totally different online and offline. You need to offer a similar quality experience and brand image to the one you are offering offline, continuing to emphasise the heritage, craftsmanship and uniqueness of your brand.

What Diamonds Can Teach Us about Digital for Luxury

To help you understand better what digital means for luxury, let me illustrate its intricacies with a simple analogy. The digital marketing strategy for your luxury brand is like a diamond; it needs a human touch and tailored techniques to realise its full potential. The strategy is all about leveraging highly skilled processes to release the internal sparkle of your brand to create mesmerising experiences for your discerning clientele.

You see, just like diamonds, there is something magical and fascinating about digital marketing for luxury brands. Think of the incredible processes that a professional with expert knowledge, equipment and tools undertakes to make a diamond shine. Imagine the weeks and months it takes to transform a rough diamond into a polished product of desire. Well, in the same way, digital for luxury brands is a long-term process that requires careful planning, a clear process, specialised skills, and discipline to make your brand shine online. I believe that when your digital brilliance illuminates your core values and messages, your brand will shine brighter than you ever imagined. These thoughts inspired my *Shine* framework, which I present in detail in part 2.

But first, let's look at some of the digital lessons you can learn from diamonds:

The Wonder of Change: from Dull to Dazzling

A rough diamond looks very much like a dull piece of glass—only when it is polished and faceted does it reach its full potential. And this process can be severe, with the transformation of a rough diamond into a precious gem sometimes meaning the diamond can lose half its weight.

In the same way, the true value of a digital marketing strategy is not revealed until after it has been crafted and refined. Luxury brands must first gain awareness of this precious digital force, shed unrefined habits and eliminate the inappropriate to allow for digital marketing to emerge as a strategic element of their entire business ecosystem.

Bespoke Craftsmanship

Diamonds come in many colors, shapes and forms. Each diamond is endowed with a personality and character uniquely its own. Yet all share certain features that allow us to compare and evaluate them.

Just like diamonds, no two digital strategies should ever be exactly the same, and you have many possible routes to building your digital roadmap. The true essence of digital for luxury is about craftsmanship, personalisation, customisation and exclusive experiences. But to succeed on your digital journey, you need discipline, hard work and specific strategic intent. Your digital strategy must reflect your own brand story while respecting digital best practices.

Flawless Clarity

Clarity measures a diamond's flaws or inclusions. The clearer the diamond, the more precious it is, and a cloudy diamond is less impressive regardless of its size. Just like diamonds, the higher the clarity of your goals, the more valuable your digital efforts will be. Those who will win the digital game are not necessarily the biggest brands but the businesses that have a clear digital vision. Indeed, digital marketing for luxury brands requires careful planning in order to yield the greatest value.

The Clear-Cut Truth

Diamonds must undergo several stages in their production before transforming into a precious gem, starting with a thorough examination of the rough diamond. During this stage the size, particular shape and relative value of the stones are determined, with all decisions dictated by the natural shape of the rough stone. If you cleave a diamond in the wrong position, the diamond can shatter and become worthless. So the one thing you should not trade off on with diamonds is the quality of the cut. Diamond cutting requires incredible amounts of patience, as well as specialised knowledge, tools, equipment and techniques.

In the same way, the quality of digital execution is key to a luxury brand avoiding a 'dilution' (or weakening) of its perceived value. In order to retain their high-end image and up-market brand values, luxury brands must ensure a flawless execution of their luxury digital marketing.

Digital success also requires a specific set of skills and a clear process. You should not embark on any digital activity without first understanding where you stand (using digital diagnostic) and where you want to be (online desirability).

Luxury with Integrity

Unfortunately, just like with diamond mining, not all digital strategies follow responsible practices. And misleading practices can damage your company's reputation in an instant. Whether you are working with an external digital agency or have an in-house digital team, if you want to succeed long term you must follow certain principles and work ethics—such as respecting copyright law and privacy policies, avoiding spammy content, clearly disclosing a brand relationship and labelling content as sponsored, and not using cloaking (that is, hiding the real destination of a link). Like most things in life, valuable customer relationships are built on trust, and this is the number one hallmark of success in the digital age.

Crafted to Perfection

When a beautiful diamond is mounted onto a ring, it is infused with a deep emotional meaning, capturing the feelings of care and pride that come with wearing such a precious piece of jewellery. Without the ring, the diamond would remain somehow 'disconnected'.

In the same way, digital transformation has to be a cross-company process and an integral part of your business strategy. You cannot build a digital marketing strategy and your tactical campaigns in silos. Your digital strategy must be fully integrated with traditional activities to offer a seamless experience across all your touchpoints. Only then will you be able to really connect with your audience.

Investments: Know Your Bling

Buying a diamond can be intimidating. What do you look for? How much should you pay?

Just like most people would recommend learning some basics before making a purchase—being able to understand, for example, the importance of the cut, carat, clarity and colour, and how they relate to a diamond's worth—you should learn to demystify the digital process so that you can invest confidently.

And in the same way as there's no ideal size for a diamond—your preference depending on your budget and taste—you should look for the best digital options for your particular brand ambitions and personality, rather than simply looking at overall scope and reach.

Digital is becoming a luxury brand's best friend. But just like in a relationship, where you have to go through certain milestones before diamond rings are exchanged, you must learn to listen to your audience and build trust before they desire your luxury brand and engage truly and deeply with you.

Perhaps digital will bring us even closer to the fundamental and original purpose of luxury—to delight the consumer. So next time you admire a diamond, think of how digital can help your brand shine with the same unprecedented brilliance.

PAUSE AND PONDER

- How can you be more nimble within your niche market? What ideas can you explore and experiment with? How can you get these to your market more quickly and then build on them in conjunction with your consumers?

- How can you build your digital strategy with the funds you have? Where can you be innovative and unique?

- What offline experiences can you bring online? How can you translate your stories to the digital space?

- How can you make your digital strategy a diamond?

CHAPTER 3

Bricks and Clicks Scrumble

LUXURY has traditionally been associated with personal service, perfect attention to detail and an immersive in-store experience that awakens all the senses—from the body language and impeccable gestures of the sales staff, to the signature scent of the boutiques and exquisite feel of the luxury products. If digital cannot (yet) play on all the senses in the same way that offline does, it can still definitely offer a compelling experience.

Remember: both offline and online marketing are primarily about human-to-human interactions (even when behind a screen). Digital is all about recognising, and heightening, these interactions.

In this chapter, I show you how the online experience can work in with consumers' offline lives—creating a 'bricks and clicks' scrumble.

The New Path to Purchase

When discussing digital strategy with luxury professionals, the topic of the importance of physical stores versus online options often comes up. I strongly believe brick-and-mortar stores will always play an important role for luxury brands. But I think we will also see an increasing number of stores acting only as a showroom, whereby people come to feel and touch the product in-store before buying it online.

DIGITAL SPARKLE

The new challenge for luxury brands is to combine the online convenience their customers demand with the high-end experience they also expect.

When paying a premium price, customers expect a unique experience, no matter whether they are online or offline, and that experience includes how a brand makes them feel right from the very beginning of their shopping journey through to the after-sales service. The way forward will thus be about delivering a unified brand experience and streamlined shopping experience that blurs the lines between the physical world and virtual world.

Luxury brands also need to remember that online experiences drive offline sales. According to research by McKinsey & Company (from July 2015), digital has become the driving force behind the luxury shopping experience, as three out of four luxury purchases are now influenced by what shoppers see, do and hear online. And this figure continues to rise.

To develop accurate digital strategies that truly resonate with your consumers' needs and desires, you must take a step back and spend time understanding the triggers and blockers that your customers experience across all the various touchpoints or interactions with your brand—including your physical stores, websites, mobile apps, ads and social networks.

For decades, marketers have been used to an orderly sequence of purchase stages—from awareness to evaluation to purchase to loyalty. But the luxury path to purchase is no longer a straightforward and linear journey, and the traditional funnel-shaped model has been scrambled. Digital channels, social media networks and mobile devices have fundamentally disrupted the way consumers interact with brands, and have made the interactions more complex and fragmented. Empowered, consumers can now start their purchase journey at any point along their decision path, and so the 'funnel' has transformed to something like a 'cycle', fed by multiple considerations along the way where the customer always takes centre stage. The following sections outline these aspects in more detail.

A Complex Path

Since purchasing a luxury item is often a journey of high consumer involvement, it's not surprising that luxury buyers have more complex paths to purchase than traditional models. Luxury shoppers research, review, stop, reconsider and seek reassurance, nimbly navigating across various touchpoints and multiple devices, resulting in a more elaborate customer journey. (According to Google, an average luxury shopper checks 10.4 sources or points of contact before he or she finally makes a purchase.)

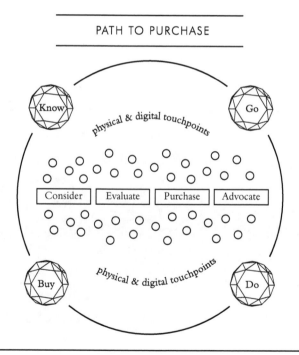

PATH TO PURCHASE

Let's illustrate this new journey with an example scenario. A woman spots a superb handbag while watching the Oscars on TV and decides she must have one. She grabs her tablet and starts reading online magazine articles featuring the various looks of this glam event. One of the articles mentions the handbag she adores and links to the brand's website. Once on the website, she watches videos showcasing the manufacturing process and browses through the full product catalogue, bookmarking the pages featuring her favourite pieces. The next day while commuting, she grabs her smartphone and resumes her activity. She downloads the brand's mobile app that lets her customise various elements of the design. She posts two bag options on her social media pages to gather reactions from her friends. With her smartphone, she locates the nearest boutique and calls to confirm they have her selected bag in stock. She visits the store and discovers she can also personalise it with her initials, and finally decides to make the purchase.

When we want to do or buy something, or learn more about something, we reflexively reach for our nearest device—and, in particular, our mobile phone. We look for information in bite-sized chunks along a larger customer journey that Google brilliantly refers to as 'micro-moments', usually revolving around four main categories of needs: 'I want to know, go, buy or do'.

DIGITAL SPARKLE

Think about all the various paths that people can take to convert. Focus on your consumers' specific needs and behaviours within each of these micro-moments, and ask 'How do we solve problems for them? How can we enhance their emotional journey?'

The new challenge for luxury brands is thus to understand user behaviours and their underlying motivations (for example, seeking status and pleasure, or confirming love and admiration for a product's performance) in order to deliver a relevant, seamless, digitally enabled experience that meets consumer needs in these intent-rich moments of their target market's choosing.

Because in just one click, shoppers can embark on a totally different path from their original intent.

An Individualised Path

A 'one-size-fits-all' approach to mapping your consumers' path to purchase no longer exists. People want to be able to choose the channel most convenient for them and expect brands to look up to them, anticipate their needs and deliver tailored experiences that harmoniously bridge the gap between online and offline channels. The modern affluent consumer is now empowered to decide how engaged he or she wants to be with the brand across the different touchpoints.

To thrive in today's complex environment, you need to invest time in analysing the data trails (or strings of data) that consumers leave behind as they seamlessly switch from one channel to another, and use this analysis to develop strategies that optimise each individual interaction. This is all about understanding what motivates your customers, and their needs and concerns. For example, a spa looking to increase its footfall during certain hours of the day could use geo-location technology to send out mobile ads to nearby consumers.

You could also use the data to analyse where consumers spend most of their time. If they spend a lot of time researching the quality of your products, perhaps you could include information focusing on this more prominently on your website and other digital channels. Or perhaps your data shows your customers are highly influenced by celebrity endorsements of your products. You could make such endorsements a bigger part of your digital strategy, and even encourage your customers to post sightings of people using your products.

Luxury brands must ensure alignment between their 'bricks and clicks' presence and enhance the emotional journey, both before and after purchase. In the end, it comes down to telling a story that resonates—

across all touchpoints. You cannot excite affluent consumers in-store and bore them online. Luxury consumers expect to be wowed in every single interaction.

Luxury brands that will be the most successful are those that best combine their online and offline channel efforts and provide a streamlined experience.

Recognising the Multi-Screen Reality

Multi-screen simply refers to the consumer habit of viewing the same content across a variety of screens, with mobile web usage fast becoming the preferred mode of internet browsing. Smartphones are now the backbone of our daily media interactions and serve as the most common starting point for online activities. But hardly anyone is faithful to one device and the majority of us use three or more devices—smartphones, laptops, tablets—on a daily basis.

In 2012, Google carried out its major study *The New Multi-screen World: Understanding Cross-platform Consumer Behavior,* which analysed the way we multi-task between media. According to this study, '90% of people move between devices to accomplish a goal, whether that's on smartphones, PCs, tablets or TV'.

Google highlighted the following two main modes of multi-screening behaviours:

- Sequential screening: where people move between devices.
- Simultaneous screening: where people use multiple devices at the same time. (Does this sound familiar? Are you often watching TV while browsing through your tablet and checking your smartphone every time you receive an email notification?)

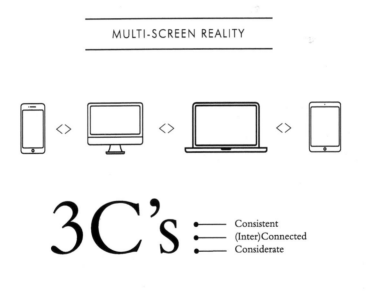

Today's consumers are constantly connected on a wide array of devices and screen sizes, and this constant connectivity and divided attention has a major impact on how people shop, communicate and consume media. Even the bedroom and bathroom are no longer screen-free sanctuaries in many households! People feel empowered and in control. They now have access to the latest information at their fingertips, no matter where they are or what time it is.

So savvy businesses know that it's absolutely essential to have a multi-screen strategy if they want to reach consumers in all the moments that matter—and this means providing a seamless experience for consumers as they move across devices. This is what affluent consumers are demanding and this applies even more so for luxury brands, where every interaction should be flawless.

This means your understanding of how customers use each device is vitally important, as is ensuring you are using the right media mix across all screens and providing a holistic experience that capitalises on each device's strengths.

DIGITAL SPARKLE

Consumers have higher-than-ever expectations and want brands to engage with them appropriately, based on the device they are using. They want to find what they want when they want it, and in as few clicks as possible.

Some requirements for providing this holistic experience in a multi-screen world are as follows:

- *Be consistent:* your brand experience and messaging should be uniform across screens, whenever and wherever someone chooses to engage with your brand.
- *Be interconnected:* think about the interactions between screens. Anticipate the most common paths and ensure that the consumers' profile and preferences are recorded across the various platforms—so that they can, for example, browse through options on their desktop and then resume their activity on their mobile phone.
- *Be considerate:* some screens are better than others at communicating particular aspects of your brand's personality, so choose these aspects accordingly. Consumers use their desktop to do in-depth research while they will often stay connected on social media with their smartphone. So make sure your message is adapted for consumption on each particular medium. For example, creating easily digestible (easy to understand) and delicious (attention-grabbing, visual and emotional) content people can literally 'snack' on while they are on the move is perfect for mobile consumption. Think of feeding your audience bite-sized but extremely filling snackable content that they can enjoy while standing in a line, commuting or waiting for a taxi. These snackable

content pieces should not just be truncated information, but intentionally designed for easy consumption on the selected devices. Tweets, Snapchat videos and Instagram posts, for instance, are good examples of snackable content—they're easily viewable and shareable on mobile devices.

Businesses need to evolve in line with these new multi-screen behaviours and find ways to be relevant to people in the context of their everyday lives. This means developing the right digital mindset to earn attention and trust through meaningful conversations, relevant content and useful services.

Indulging in the Online Luxury Retail Experience

The traditional wisdom among luxury brands used to be that e-commerce or e-retail (as I prefer to call it in the context of luxury) and selling through multi-brand retail websites was not appropriate for these brands. Many simply believed that people wouldn't buy expensive things online. But the success of luxury online fashion retailer Net-A-Porter and its merger with Yoox, as well as the increased visibility of platforms like Farfetch or Gilt and their like, have proven them wrong.

E-retail is the fastest-growing sales channel for luxury, according to Bain & Company's *Global Luxury Goods Worldwide Market Study*, issued in late 2014. If, at the time of writing, the majority of luxury purchases still happen offline, online shopping is certainly gaining some momentum. BNP Paribas analyst Luca Solca says, 'Digital could be "the next China"' for luxe brands, 'adding about $43 billion in sales through 2020'.

E-retail sites are opening the doors to the world's best luxury boutiques—boutiques that are open 24/7, without geographical borders. So this channel is both the next big challenge and a big opportunity for luxury brands.

Many luxury brands are still hesitant to fully embrace e-retail as part of their distribution strategy, however. Fearful of losing a feeling of exclusivity, but knowing they should offer some sort of digital experience, other luxury brands are somewhere in-between, only providing a limited online boutique.

The Altagamma-McKinsey Digital Luxury Experience Observatory identified three digital archetypes within each luxury category, along with the following characteristics:

- *Plugged-in pro:*
  - diversified retail strategy (using both mono- and multi-brand stores)
  - 360° use of digital, from social to fully fledged online store.
- *Selective e-tailer:*
  - tight retail control (monobrand sites only)

- opportunistic use of digital as entry point for aspirational customers:
  * use of digital as a marketing channel
  * online store for entry-level products only.
- *Hesitant holdout:*
  - tight control of retail (monobrand stores only)
  - use of online as showroom only, rather than a point of sale.

Against this (and especially for those 'hesitant holdouts') here are some of the reasons luxury brands could benefit from increasing their e-retail offering:

- The number of affluent online shoppers is growing fast, especially for affordable luxury goods.
- Young professionals and affluent middle-aged consumers are increasingly comfortable with buying high-priced items online and on mobile, enjoying in particular the convenience it brings.
- While discovery is still a large part of digital engagement, more and more consumers are willing to make transactions online.
- Millennial consumers are very comfortable in the online environment.
- Entering a physical luxury retail store can sometimes be intimidating.

- For niche luxury brands with limited boutiques, e-retail can mean a broader distribution and instant access to consumers worldwide.

Given the exponential segment growth, luxury brands should consider taking advantage of this opportunity—and a key way to do so is to offer an enticing online experience.

While buying online might not yet be as glamorous as strolling and shopping on Avenue des Champs-Élysées or Rodeo Drive, done right, luxury brands' e-retail sites can be a sophisticated experience—and part 2 of this book offers more on this.

PAUSE AND PONDER

- What are your consumers' pain points with your brand? How can you help move them along their path and eliminate friction?

- Do you know a typical 'path to purchase' for your customers? What do their various paths to purchase look like? Where do customers abandon the shopping process?

- What are the main devices customers use when engaging with you online? Is your strategy best suited to these kinds of devices?

- What touchpoints are most effective in influencing a purchase?

- Where do you sit among the three digital archetypes? Plugged-in pro, selective e-tailer or hesitant holdout?

CHAPTER 4

The New Affluent Consumers

WHILE being affluent can mean different things in different parts of the world, finding common characteristics can help you better target this discerning consumer base.

Historically, luxury brands were exclusively reserved for the privileged few—the rich and the elite. The profile of a luxury shopper thus used to be fairly clear and simple, and most people could easily imagine a man or woman who owned a lavish property, flaunted a Rolex watch and travelled first class with their Louis Vuitton luggage.

Nowadays, however, luxury is no longer reserved for the rich classes. Luxury also appeals to less affluent consumers, even if they are likely to only afford selected luxury items. Therefore, segmentation approaches based only on criteria such as wealth and income are insufficient. This chapter helps you break down, and so target, your consumer base more effectively.

Profiles of the New Affluent Consumers

Not all affluent consumers are the same, and today's luxury shoppers are a much more diverse group than in the past. Their motives have become highly differentiated, and they also have wide-ranging tastes and different sets of values. When developing strategies to reach these affluent customers—what I have called the 'new affluent consumers'—it's also important to understand that many levels of wealth exist, from those who are 'comfortable' to those who are the ultra rich of this world.

With that in mind—and even though I am not a fan of personas (which I often find too clichéd)—let me introduce the four profiles of luxury shoppers defined by Epsilon in *The New Face of Luxury*, which I believe nicely segments luxury buyers into different consumer groups. The report also looks at the immediate value of these shoppers versus their overall capacity to purchase.

Here's how Epsilon breaks down the new affluent consumers and luxury shoppers:

- *'Aspirational' shopper:* this type of shopper desires to own pieces from a brand, but does not have the means to do so on a regular basis. This customer shops mostly from outlets or online members-only discount boutiques, or purchases lower-ticket designer brand items such as cosmetics.

- *'Moments of Wealth' shopper:* this shopper may save for a specific piece from a particular luxury brand, but does not purchase from the brand frequently. This shopper tends to make one-off purchases over a long span of time.
- *'Dressed for the Part' shopper:* this shopper purchases luxury items to give off the appearance of being someone who lives a luxury lifestyle, but does not have the financial resources to be a true luxury buyer. This fashionista shopper devotes most of his or her spend to fashion, accessories or a car, rather than an expensive home.
- *'True Luxe' shopper:* the 'True Luxe' shopper has the means to purchase luxury items at will without concern for finances. This shopper purchases from luxury retailers frequently throughout the year.

Knowing what sort of shopper makes up your target consumer segments means you can design your digital strategy appropriately. Say, for example, you wanted a strategy that targeted the segment you have identified as 'aspirational shoppers'. In this case, you'd design a social media campaign that highlighted your more entry-level, but iconic, items. If you wanted to focus on your 'true luxe' customers, on the other hand, you might offer them an exclusive sign-in 'members only' page on your website, which provides details of upcoming new releases and exclusive showings, or special 'behind-the-scenes' scoops.

DIGITAL SPARKLE

Defining common characteristics that break your target consumers into segments that think and behave in a similar fashion can help you better communicate and engage with these various affluent consumers.

Affluent Consumers: Global, Mobile and Digital

As well as looking at your market segmentation, you also need to understand how the luxury market has been disrupted by younger generations and changing consumer habits. An industry once dominated by middle-aged affluent buyers is now seeing a new generation of young and affluent consumers: the millennials. This generation, born between 1980 and 2000, is expected to be the largest generational segment—and most valuable demographic—in the luxury consumer market by around 2018 to 2020.

Digital Fluency

The millennial generation is the first of its kind to have grown up in the technology era. With a firm grasp of digital technology, wealthy millennials are bringing new expectations and new experiences to the market for luxury. Young people choose and buy differently. Millennials aren't driven by traditional status symbols and instead splurge on discretionary items. Younger consumers also live and breathe in social networks; they are used to communicating with each other about the brands they prefer via various social media channels. These days, what you say about yourself is less important; what matters is what people say about your brand. Businesses that do not cultivate a transparent, authentic conversation with their customers will struggle.

As mentioned, the internet is also dramatically changing media consumption habits. The new affluent consumers live in a multi-screen environment: from TV, to desktops, to tablets and mobiles. They could be defined as living digitally infused lifestyles.

These consumers are inundated with information and choices, and they are extensively and increasingly using the internet and digital channels to investigate and research brands, discover and make luxury purchases online, and connect and share with people with similar outlooks. They are more selective, more pragmatic, more demanding and more careful about what luxuries they buy and how much they spend.

Borderless Consumers

Another new phenomenon among luxury consumers is cross-pollination of luxury spending. In other words, the number of global consumers acquiring high-end goods when travelling abroad and expecting coherent brand experiences whatever the location is growing. For example, many Chinese consumers prefer to buy luxury goods in Europe (even if similar products are readily available in their home country) to avoid high domestic prices and taxes, or to gain access to products ahead of their release in their home country.

In an attempt to harmonise the staggering price difference that resulted from the weakened euro, European luxury brands have started to rebalance their pricing models internationally, with some luxury brands such as Chanel and Patek Philippe attempting to address the price differential between Asia and Europe. For companies with a global customer base, a simplified pricing structure can also protect brands from a flourishing gray market—whereby travellers buy handbags in Europe, for example, and resell them in Asia—and discourage fakes. In the current digital context this is even more important, because pricing is more transparent and it has become easier for consumers to find third-party luxury sellers online.

As rents at the premier malls and high street locations continue to rise, some luxury brands are also reshaping their retail footprint to optimise return on capital. Luxury brands will inevitably need to take a strategic look at their store portfolios and fully understand the role of their brick-and-mortar boutiques in a world of growing digitisation.

These trends mean, when developing digital strategies, you need to understand the scope and extent of the digital world, which stretches far beyond your local environment.

Mobile-First Generation

Technology is more embedded than ever in consumers' daily lives. For an increasing number of people, mobile is the only screen looked at, and often the 'go-to' device for the web. According to Gartner, 'By 2018, more than 50 per cent of users will use a tablet or smartphone first for all online activities'.

And the importance of mobile connectivity will continue to rise, driven by smartphones, tablets and wearable technologies. The new affluent consumers are increasingly using mobile devices to search for products and store locations while on the go—while commuting, dining, or shopping. These connected customers present a powerful engagement opportunity for luxury brands, but this also means businesses and brands will need to become better publishers, agile publishers who can create polished 'snackable' content that's easily consumed on mobile devices. Your focus needs to be on understanding your audience's mobile habits and being capable of faster adaptation, shorter lead times and real-time marketing to deliver mobile-optimised content that is both relevant and engaging. Mobile is thus an essential component to a luxury brand's marketing strategy.

In this new modern context, luxury brands must become relationship managers for mobile consumers.

Tailoring Your Brand and Your Product

As luxury consumers become more diverse and discerning, they are increasingly seeking personalisation and bespoke products and services. In turn, this means luxury brands are starting to recognise that to keep customers interested in their products, they have to make them feel unique.

To stay relevant, luxury brands will have to deliver and look for ways to tailor their marketing efforts to each consumer's need for individuality. Personalisation plays on consumer sentiment and is an essential part of the experiential services associated with luxury brands.

As an example of this, Louis Vuitton launched its personalised 'Mon Monogram' service in 2010, while in 2011 Hermès created 'Custom Silk Corner', which allowed consumers to make their own versions of its scarves.

Burberry, too, has put consumers at the centre of its brand with the Burberry Monogramming Service, available both online and in select stores. From the heritage cashmere scarf, poncho and My Burberry perfume bottle to the now iconic trench coat, customers can truly personalise their desired products with up to three initials in the Burberry font. The monogramming online tool on Burberry.com allows customers to preview the monogramming using their desired initials in real time before they press the 'buy' button.

DIGITAL SPARKLE

The new wealth world is changing. That's a fact. Affluent consumers now come from various cultures and social classes, and consume media and information in endlessly varying ways. In this new context, luxury brands must leverage digital to engage consumers across multiple channels—harmoniously.

As demographics change and evolve, it is crucial for luxury brands to have a clear understanding of how to reach and impact the emerging affluent consumers. To stay relevant, you need to weave your brand stories around the individual desires and aspirations of your customers and prospects. This does not mean presenting an entirely different company to each customer; instead, this is about offering experiences that are contextual to customers' personal intentions.

Targeting the Empowered Consumer

Digital has shifted power into the hands of the consumers, bringing with it more transparency and empowering consumers with extensive information and more choice, whenever and wherever they want it. A swipe, a tap or a double click and we're face-to-face with the finer things in life. With this significant shift comes a pressing need to market to the modern affluent consumer in an innovative way.

Digital—and in particular social media—has evened the playing field by giving consumers increased access to both information and products previously unavailable to them. Digital has also opened the door to creators, sharers and influencers.

Today's affluent consumers are more educated and more purposeful, and they're looking for a more understated expression of their lifestyle. They are embracing brands that tell them great stories about quality and unique craftsmanship, while reflecting their personal values. (See chapter 7 for more on engaging customers through great digital storytelling.)

As consumers become more knowledgeable, the challenge for businesses is to meet their raised expectations. Today, brands cannot just push out the 'right' message. They need to also listen and react to what consumers are saying back to them.

More than ever, reaching your target audience today is about being relevant. So it's crucial to understand the needs, beliefs and motivations of the new affluent consumers. The more clearly you understand them, as distinct from earlier models of wealth, the more effectively you will be able to deeply connect with them and unlock your brand's full potential.

To succeed, luxury brands must provide a personable, interactive and targeted experience—a strategy I'll expand on throughout part 2.

PAUSE AND PONDER

- Do you know the profile(s) of your luxury shoppers?
- Do you know the breakdown of your current and target market?
- Do you understand why your customers buy your product or service? I mean, really understand what makes them buy from you?
- What pain points (such as time pressure or social pressure...) do your customers have and how does your product or service address those?
- Are you offering some level of personalisation or bespoke products and services?
- Do you know the general online sentiments relating to your brand? Are you listening to what people say about your brand online? Do you regularly 'Google' your brand name, product name and industry? Are you pleased with what you read?
- Have you put an online monitoring system in place?

PART 2

THE HOW

'People will forget what you said,
people will forget what you did,
but people will never forget
how you made them feel.'

—MAYA ANGELOU

CHAPTER 5

A Digital Framework to Make Your Brand *Shine*

THE internet, mobile web platforms and social media are forever changing the business landscape. Digital opens the routes to amazing opportunities for innovative luxury brands—if you know *how*. In part 1, I covered some of the key elements that constitute the new luxury environment, and explained why digital transformation is a crucial source of growth for luxury brands. It is also the case that today's luxury consumers have higher expectations from luxury brands in terms of online innovation and that they will easily move away from a brand if it fails to deliver up to their expectations. Digital media enables you to reach consumers where they are but any communication is now on the consumer's terms.

Whatever stage of growth your company is in now, you need to embark on your digital journey as soon as possible. Many possible routes to building your digital roadmap are available, but for your strategy to succeed, you require discipline, hard work and specific strategic intent. The journey may vary from one brand to another, but one thing is consistent across all: once you begin, you should maintain the momentum and never stop.

You are reading this book so I am sure you want to fully embrace digital and play by the new rules. However, I know that making it happen can be confusing. So to make your ride a little bit smoother, I'm going to share some insights and advice that will help you define the structure of your digital strategy and develop the business culture to best grow your business in the new digital era.

Over the next few chapters I provide everything you need to unlock the right digital mindset for your luxury brand.

Digital Audit: Understanding Where You Stand Now

Given the fast-moving nature of digital and its direct implications across your business, staying current is critical. Even though I know that interpreting the impact of digital on your business can be overwhelming, I am always surprised to hear people jumping head first into digital implementation without a clear understanding of where they actually stand (now) and where they want to end up (then). Some luxury professionals have even confessed to me that their decisions related to digital were often based on intuition and instinct rather than an informed strategy.

However, knowing your skills and understanding your attitudes and where you are now can help you better craft a strategy that builds from your strengths and acknowledges and addresses your weaknesses. Plus such a strategy can enable you to allocate your time and energy in ways that will be most effective. Only with an accurate view of your current situation can you design a tailored plan—or course of action—that best meets the specific needs of your business and sets clear and realistic goals for your brand, and the right benchmarks to evaluate the success of your plan.

The first step towards a successful business transformation is always assessment (or running your diagnostics), and a digital audit is a comprehensive and systematic process of examining the overall performance of your digital marketing—or, put simply, a study of your brand's online presence, both as a standalone analysis and vis-à-vis the competition. This initial stage is essential because it will inform your investments and initiatives and help you create a much, much better digital strategy.

A comprehensive digital audit requires you to really deep dive into your business, so in this section I have highlighted some fundamental questions that can help you get a snapshot of your digital status.

A digital marketing audit can evaluate numerous metrics but I have listed here some of the key ones to get you started.

I developed this simple assessment framework to help businesses self-diagnose their current digital reality, discover their strengths, highlight their under-performing digital assets and recurring pitfalls, and uncover the opportunities that digital change will provide.

The diagnostic checklist within this framework brings together a lot of my thinking into one simple question-and-answer process, helping you quickly identify key opportunity areas for competitive differentiation and pointing out current gaps and blind spots.

Remember: it may also be worthwhile to involve a professional digital agency to perform the digital audit, because this agency can look into your overall digital strategy from a fresh perspective and push your team to be disciplined and pragmatic. (See chapter 11 for more on working with an agency.)

Whether you're engaging an agency or doing it alone, put on your thinking cap and gather your key stakeholders as you follow this simple digital audit process:

1. *Collect:* gather information from various sources (including web analytics, competitor analysis, customer feedback, surveys and social media listening tools).
2. *Review:* evaluate data that truly matter. What do you count as a 'success'? Make sure to define your evaluation criteria based on

what metrics are important for your business. This step is about understanding where you are doing well and where you are not performing so well.

3. *Understand:* make sense of the data collected and highlight key issues.

4. *Take action:* with all this information in hand, you can now articulate your strengths and areas requiring improvement and plan your strategy accordingly.

This may seem a little simplistic, so let me break it down further for you with an audit checklist. Work through the following with your agency and/or key stakeholders:

- *Now:* where do you stand presently? What do you currently do online?
- *Then:* where do you want to be?
- *Obstacles:* what's in the way?
- *Readiness:* what resources and foundations do you need? Consider the following:
  - Do you have the internal resources (people, budget, time) and the necessary digital literacy to establish a strong presence and represent your business and brand(s) well?
  - Is integrating digital capabilities into your business operating model a top priority on your strategic agenda?
  - Do you have the full support and engagement of your senior leadership?

- Have you thought through the implications of digital technologies and do you understand your need to adapt your business model?
- What is the current organisational comfort level with technology?
- *Reach:* what is your exposure across organic and paid digital channels? Consider:
  - Where do you reach your audience, and how do you make this happen?
  - What is your current presence across owned (for example, your brand website, native apps or social media networks you control), paid (display ads, sponsorships, and paid search) and earned (online word of mouth, such as mentions, shares, reviews or content picked up by third parties) channels?
- *Integration:* how do your online and offline experiences work together? Look at the following:
  - Do you offer a streamlined experience to customers across online and offline channels—wherever, whenever and however they contact your business?
  - Are your digital engagement activities deployed cross-functionally?
- *Measurement:* how do you work out whether your strategies are working? For example:
  - Do you have reporting protocols in place?

- Have you defined clear metrics to evaluate your digital activities?
- Do you have feedback loops in place?
- Are reports analysed and acted upon?
- *Website:* is this working effectively? Consider the following:
  - Do you have a mobile-friendly website?
  - Do you regularly update your website?
  - Do you have quality links pointing to your website?
  - Is your website user-friendly?
- *Searchability:* can people easily find your website in search results? And can people easily find valuable information about your brand online?
- *Social media:* is this working for your brand as well as it could? Consider:
  - Have you devoted the resources, both financial and human, to creating and maintaining a powerful social media presence on all relevant networks?
  - What social media platforms is your organisation on?
  - How frequently do you post, and what type of content do you post?
  - Do you have an overarching social media strategy set out?
  - Are your social media channels engaging?
- *Content:* do you include relevant curated and/or created content? For example:
  - Do you have a content strategy in place?

- Do you have a content or editorial calendar in place?
- Have you identified trusted sources for your curated content?
- Do you know which types of messages are performing best with your audience?
- *Email and customer relationship management:* is this working as well as it could be? For example:
  - Do you send out e-newsletters? If so, how frequently?
  - Do you personalise each email—for example, with a 'hello [name]'?
  - Do you track your performances (such as open rate and click-through rate) and, if so, how does your analysis inform your next e-newsletter?

Once you've worked through the preceding checklist, perhaps you're able to give your brand's digital strategy top marks in most areas. If you're like most luxury brands, however, you've likely found your current strategy wanting. Don't despair: in the following section I outline my framework for digital transformation.

Shine with Your Digital Transformation

I'm here to tell you that it doesn't matter how big or old your brand is, or what sector or industry you operate in—digital transformation is inevitable. And, indeed, businesses everywhere are recognising the pressing need to coordinate, plan for, and implement digital marketing efforts to stay relevant in our increasingly connected society. But very few know how transformational digital needs to be and what it actually encompasses.

DIGITAL SPARKLE

Luxury business owners need to recognise that digital is a worthwhile long-term investment and not just a short-term tactical initiative. This means you need to understand the scope of digital and how to allot a place for it within your internal organisation.

Developing the right digital process can be daunting. New digital marketing channels appear every day, and tools and platforms that were cutting edge yesterday can fast become obsolete today. Chances are, if you're reading this book, you're struggling to keep up with the latest technologies and are not sure how to go about marketing your premium or luxury brand online.

Talking to many business owners and CEOs, I was surprised to hear that, although they understood they needed to 'go digital', most of them did not have a clear idea of the fundamental business outcomes they wished to achieve by doing so. Many businesses are like this:

they pursue digital initiatives without really thinking things through. When I asked, for example, for details on their primary digital strategy, most business owners told me they had created a Facebook page, and not much else. Perhaps an email blast every so often to a limited list of subscribers, a nice looking website and … voila! Their digital strategy was complete.

But the digital reality is much more complex. And while change is always confusing, digital has brought a whole new level of complexity, because everything is happening so fast. But even within this constant change, some consistencies emerge. Digital is not just about what you do to attract traffic, but also about the type of experiences you create for the consumers across multiple screens, and how you build long-term relationships with them.

I have noticed that many businesses invest in the wrong channels or develop digital tactics in silos. Businesses also often get lost in the tools and technical jargon. As the volume of digital channels and tools increases, issues of integration and aggregation become more important than ever.

Through a decade of working as a marketing strategist and advising premium businesses and luxury brands on how to leverage digital, I have observed how brands assimilate new concepts and embrace new trends. And I have realised that, while many marketers tend to concentrate on tactics and tools—which, by their very nature, come and go—the focus should be shifted to understanding the overarching digital ecosystem and what it means for your business. This is where my *Shine* framework comes in.

Understanding the Shine *Framework*

When talking with business owners and marketers, I've found that the most memorable takeaways for people are usually frameworks. Frameworks give clarity and can help structure actions, and also provide a solid foundation and easily understood guidance for future strategies. So I developed the *Shine* framework to help luxury SMEs and niche businesses plan and manage their digital marketing activities in a more structured way.

Every business has its own path to becoming digitally successful, depending on its unique set of needs and priorities. But while each business will have different objectives, the fundamental attributes are the same.

The purpose of this framework is to put the most important aspects of digital marketing into a model and, ultimately, help you manage and improve results from your digital marketing. I hope it will help simplify your approach to reviewing the performance of your digital marketing and taking actions to improve its effectiveness. The *Shine* framework presents a set of principles that need to be adopted in order to successfully embrace digital, and provides specific goals that can serve as benchmarks for progress made against each of the principle areas.

The *Shine* model provides a simple set of prerequisites to adopting the right digital mindset. It's a constellation that connects the five main components of digital marketing and puts your niche in the center.

The *Shine* mnemonic summarises these five key pillars or key building blocks that luxury businesses need to hone to achieve their 'digital sweet spot'. The five pillars are **S**trategy, **H**olistic implementation, **I**ntelligence, **N**imbleness and **E**ngagement.

THE SHINE MODEL

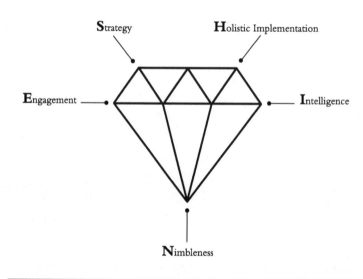

S for Strategy

First and foremost, to be successful in digital you need to set down the right foundations, and achieving this starts with the right strategy. A digital strategy is a strategy for servicing the new digital consumer, and developing such a strategy seems an obvious place to start, but this critical component is often overlooked. And lacking a clear business direction, vision and roadmap that define the digital way forward is often the reason businesses fail in digital marketing. Their ill-thought-out digital initiatives drive up marketing spending but produce only marginal enhancements—so these businesses then start claiming that digital just does not work for them.

Instead, businesses need to define what it is that they are trying to achieve for their premium or luxury brand, product or service in the digital space, and develop a specific process. Taking this time upfront can dramatically improve your results. The strategy should focus on concrete actions, and should identify both practical, short-term digital priorities (which address the immediate issues) and long-term goals (which establish processes for adapting to future changes in consumer behaviours) that are sophisticated, informed and forward-thinking.

Short-term goals could be things like assigning a dedicated person to schedule and manage social media feeds, or to add 200 new names to the email subscriber list for your company's e-newsletter over a defined period. Long-term goals are typically the most meaningful because they usually relate to the 'big picture' for the brand; an example could be to increase your brand's online visibility.

I discuss strategy in much more detail in chapter 6, which covers finding your niche, and in chapter 7, on engaging your customers.

H for Holistic Implementation

A great strategy means very little without effective implementation. During this creation phase, you need to decide what channels and technology make sense to leverage for *your* business, and ensure this implementation is integrated across all aspects of the business. An integrated implementation is key to creating—and sustaining—seamless customer experiences. As already mentioned, businesses can no longer view digital marketing as a siloed function, and by adopting an integrated approach to digital you will deliver far more value than initiatives launched in silos. For luxury brands in particular, where brands are aiming to retain their high-end image, conveying a holistic and consistent brand identity across all channels, both online and offline, is especially important. Just like with your strategy, the quality of the execution is key in avoiding a digital 'dilution' of your luxury brand's perceived value.

Chapters 8 and 9 look at implementation more deeply, where I cover building your online presence and taking advantage of social media.

I for Intelligence

It's always important to measure the effectiveness of your activities, and I've found that defining clear key performance indicators (KPIs) before you embark on any new project helps ensure you deliver within your budgets, deadlines and business imperatives.

Analytics from your business and the competition can help you diagnose deficiencies in specific channels in your marketing mix and help you drive a continual improvement of your customer experience —and, ultimately, achieve your desired outcomes.

Consumers expect highly personalised experiences when interacting with luxury brands, so spending time collecting and understanding data (for example, average time spent on your website, as well as demographics, interests and sources of traffic) and closely monitoring the response to your marketing programs is even more crucial. Using the increasing volume of data and insights (both qualitative and quantitative) available, you can then understand (and anticipate) customers' behaviours and map your customers' journeys in detail.

Such analysis and mapping help you discover distinctive ways to provide real value to your customers. And remember: in this 'noisy' connected world, you need to be relevant to your consumers in order to stand out. So ensure you have the right people and processes in place to uncover all the ways you engage with your customers and measure the effectiveness of those engagements.

I cover gathering intelligence in chapter 10, where I devote the whole chapter to the topic.

N for Nimbleness

In order to be successful, you must continually evaluate your performance and adapt quickly to the fast-moving pace of digital—constantly trialling new approaches to help you gain or retain your audiences. Businesses need to become more agile and more responsive to changes in demand.

Because new technologies are always being introduced and older ones reviewed, it's important for businesses to constantly seek to optimise their digital efforts. No longer can you simply plan and implement your digital strategy, and then forget about it. Instead, one of the core principles of the digital context is to test, improve, test again, refine again and so on.

Zara, through defying the conventional wisdom and time frame of the supply chain in the fashion industry, is a great example of an agile brand. Zara is able to design, produce and deliver a new garment and have it on display in its stores worldwide in a mere two weeks. Even though luxury brands are not (and should not) be expected to compromise on craftsmanship and their timeless value by cutting supply time frames to this extreme, I include this example as a way to illustrate how luxury brands should look at their digital marketing strategies. Digital nimbleness is all about being able to act fast and adapt to demand by exploiting consumer and cultural changes.

I provide tips on improving your brand's nimbleness in chapter 11.

E for Engagement

Traditionally, the foundational elements of the marketing discipline were its 4Ps (Product, Price, Place and Promotion). The new rules of digital engagement, however, are demanding an augmented approach to these elements. Today strategy is also about Content, Context (that is, relevance, timeliness and personalisation matter), Connection and Conversation. These 4Cs can actually be summed up with one word: Engagement. Your customer relationship, and the way you engage your customers and they engage with you, is key—whatever the medium or channel.

Many businesses still don't understand this, focusing on exposure over engagement. I often hear brands concerned about the reach of their social media page, for example, and so they focused mainly on chasing likes and followers. But having thousands of highly engaged customers could be way more powerful than having millions of disengaged fans.

Premium and luxury brands derive their worth from the emotional content and meaning they convey, and delivering engaging customer experiences drives sales and long-term loyalty. Gone are the days where consumers were leaning back and receiving one-way brand messages. The growth in connectivity and social media networks, and the rise in the number of mobile devices, have empowered consumers, and they now decide if, when, where and how they interact with brands. (In a recent study, Google and Advertising Age referred to this trend as heralding the 'Participation Age'.)

In the sea of digital noise, it's now more important than ever to pay attention to customer engagement. Indeed, placing your brand's strategic emphasis on the creation of valuable relationships could mean the difference between boring monologues and powerful conversations.

Engagement is all about being relevant in each and every stage of the consumer journey, and delivering against a desired experience and continuously improving the quality of those interactions. I talk about engagement in much more detail in chapter 7, but this is something for you to be thinking about through all steps in the *Shine* process.

For now, keep in mind these points when engaging with luxury consumers:

- *Personalisation is key:* more and more people are expecting to be empowered to achieve high levels of personalisation for the products or experiences they buy, based on their specific behaviours and actions. Leverage data and insights for your brand to provide relevant information and bespoke experiences. One of my clients from Japan, Regency Group, specialises in crafting bespoke itineraries based on each client's specific requests and their knowledge of the client's dream destination. They offer highly customised experiences that meet customers' individual needs—from private Japanese Sake tasting and special Kaiseki dinners in a secret and hidden place to customised visits of historical sites after public hours. Whatever they recommend comes with a personal stamp of approval.

- *Be everywhere your customers are:* today's luxury consumers are multichannel and multi-screen shoppers. The distinction between being 'on' or 'off' no longer exists. Consumers can be researching on their smartphone while shopping in-store. They can be watching television while chatting on social media or browsing through their tablets or print magazines. This means you need to be present consistently across all these channels.

- *Empower consumers to co-create:* allowing consumers to actively be part of the product development process, right from initial conception, to creating their own product to purchase, can enhance further levels of engagement by encouraging feelings of product ownership. Caratell, for example, a Singapore-based boutique luxury jeweller, crafts unique jewellery pieces and personally involves the consumer on every step of the process, from the design right down to the choice of materials, finishes and gems. Now that's the ultimate bespoke experience.

- *Understand individual customer needs:* with deep customer knowledge you will be able to develop services to solve individual customer's problems and, therefore, drive deeper connections and sustained loyalty and engagement.

Aligning Your Digital Strategy with Your Business Objectives

As already mentioned, historically, luxury brands have been slow to embrace digital. And although luxury brands are now starting to recognise the significant opportunities that digital creates, both in attracting new affluent consumers and connecting with existing luxury shoppers, the problem remains that many don't know how to align a digital strategy with their overall business objectives and marketing strategy.

When I meet a potential client for the first time, I always ask them, 'What goals and objectives are you trying to achieve through digital?' Often the answer—or lack of a detailed answer—is rather surprising. Many clients don't have an answer ready because they haven't actually thought one through. Too often, digital is perceived as just this extra 'channel' that we must include in the marketing mix in some way or another, and this lack of alignment results in a cacophony of disconnected and inconsistent activities.

Rethinking Marketing

Traditional in-house marketing teams are still deeply rooted in what they know and what they have been doing successfully for years.

Digital is disrupting, however, and requires a broad array of new skills—and, as Adobe highlighted in its report *Digital Roadblock: Marketers struggle to reinvent themselves*, most marketers don't know how to actually go about it.

Developing cool digital initiatives and tacking them onto a traditional business infrastructure and mindset will not work long term. Businesses must strategically build their brand in an integrated approach that aligns with their overall business functions.

Digital is fundamentally changing the nature of marketing and business. To succeed, marketers need to adapt to the new reality. Marketers who are willing to explore new things, learn, experiment with new capabilities and embrace digital will reap all the benefits.

DIGITAL SPARKLE

To be successful, businesses must start their digital transformation with a vision—a vision for the business in the digital age, rather than just a digital action plan. This is an important distinction.

It's vital for all marketers and C-suite executives to understand and articulate the importance of digital to their organisation, because doing so is a first step towards embracing change. This does not mean they need to increase their technical knowledge and understand how everything actually works, but it does mean they need to understand digital capability and how it can benefit the business in its entirety.

Many premium business owners and senior managers in luxury brands lack understanding around what digital actually is. Often, they fail to realise how digital has changed the way people behave, and so fail to grasp how incompatible their current processes might have become. If the concept of e-commerce (at least at the surface level) is usually understood, the other digital channels and strategies are not so much—I discovered during my multiple discussions with luxury marketers, for example, that they often understand the detrimental impact of a negative social media post seen by millions, but were less clear on the beneficial value that digital can bring when done right.

Removing Silos

Another main problem is that many businesses use digital channels developed in isolation, resulting in inconsistency and dislocation between digital and traditional messages. Again, everything comes down to your customer and their experience, and businesses must focus on delivering a seamless cross-channel engagement model for their stakeholders. The lines between digital and traditional marketing have been blurred—forever. It's time to bridge both the online and offline worlds.

Digital is too often managed as a side game—as nothing more than an add-on to a brand's existing offering—and in a mostly reactive manner, with little or no proper strategy incorporated into the process. My experience in different industries and countries has taught me that in order to be successful, digital transformation has to be a cross-company process and an integral part of the business strategy. Without a clear direction, you are setting yourself up for failure. Developing a customer journey map across all brand interactions can help you see digital in context and the functionalities it should hold within your business. Think of this customer journey map as a timeline that showcases the various stages a customer passes through when interacting with your brand or a picture of their behaviours. This process also helps you highlight shortcomings and identify where the business is failing to meet the needs and expectations of your customers. Remember: to thrive in the digital age, marketing must adopt a continuous improvement strategy, and be more nimble, engaging and participatory than in years past.

To get started on this process, simply put your customer glasses on and leave behind your outdated assumptions. For each stage, list your customers':

- *Actions:* think of all your different touchpoints. How do they search for information? Where do they look for it?
- *Questions:* consider their main challenges and problems. What motivates them to act?

- *Emotions or feelings:* imagine how each touchpoint makes them feel. Are they feeling engaged or frustrated?

Once you have developed your customer journey map, talk to as many customers as possible to ensure it is accurate.

Digital Craftsmanship: a Roadmap for Luxury Brands

The characteristics highlighted in my *Shine* model should be at the core of everything you do that involves digital. Working closely as an end-to-end digital partner for various premium and luxury brands, both emerging and established, I understand the special attention that these brands require. Just like you need to spend time on crafting your bespoke and unique products and experiences, you also need to spend time creating a bespoke digital strategy for your brand.

I also noticed, in particular, that along with a clear framework for developing a strategy, what many luxury niche businesses were then missing was a clear path to digital transformation. So to end this chapter I would like to share with you my five-step roadmap to implementing the *Shine* framework and building a solid foundation on which to build your strategy.

Here's your roadmap to digital craftsmanship:

1. *Understand:* undertake assessment and research to identify the barriers and opportunities that exist online for your brand, considering:
   - your digital readiness

- your niche and how you can build your digital strategy based on an understanding of your customers' needs and how they engage with you, looking at:
  - Who is your niche?
  - What's the central question of your niche?
  - What's your consumer's digital footprint?
- your environment, looking at:
  - How do your competitors do in terms of the *Shine* model?
  - What do your competitors do right or wrong?
  - What are the latest trends and innovations in your industry?

2. *Create:* craft your bespoke strategy, keeping the following in mind:
   - align your digital marketing strategy with your overall business strategy
   - use research findings to develop key business objectives that you want to achieve through digital
   - articulate the intangible through storytelling.

3. *Implement:* ensure a flawless presence and design first-class user experiences.

4. *Amplify:* share, recycle and repack your content and your winning campaigns across multiple touchpoints.

5. *Analyse and learn:* measure your performance and refine and iterate using the following:
   - set periodic KPIs

- track, measure and evaluate digital performance
- develop clear goals and relevant metrics, and rely on data to quickly adapt.

Remember: don't be discouraged; get excited. You have the opportunity to access massive potential to grow your luxury business through digital innovation.

DIGITAL CRAFTSMANSHIP ROADMAP

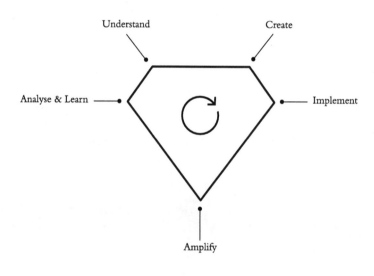

PAUSE AND PONDER

- How are your digital marketing goals looking? Where do you plan to go ultimately? What is your purpose? What are your guiding principles?

- How can you use this to create your customer journey map?

- Are your digital objectives aligned with your business goals?

- Is your business ready to embrace the *Shine* model?

CHAPTER 6

Defining Your Niche

EVERY business needs to start with and evolve around its niche audience, and in today's economy, having a well-defined target audience is more important than ever. For luxury brands in particular, identifying a niche (customer segmentation and product differentiation) is crucially important in enabling you to serve your market more precisely and successfully build your brand. People want things that are made 'just for people just like them', which means small businesses can effectively compete with large companies by finding a distinctive space and targeting the right niche. To be successful, luxury marketers need an in-depth knowledge of their affluent consumers to meet their specific needs and aspirations.

Clearly understanding your niche audience then helps you understand what technologies and digital channels you should invest in, because you can look closely at how these tools can help fulfill the inherent needs of your audience. Think of demographics, psychographics and behavioural patterns. Only when you understand your customers intimately—not simply who they are in terms of demographics but also how they behave and what motivates them, their passions and priorities—will you be able to attend to them effectively.

All industries have niche segments that can be explored, and so all provide the opportunity for you to create a distinctive brand space in the minds of your consumers—if you do it right. And doing it right is all about understanding the benefits and values that your customers desire.

Many niche brands punch above their weight by knowing their customers well—for example, Kwanpen, a family-owned enterprise based in Singapore, has carved a niche for itself with its exclusive lines of colourful leather goods made from crocodile skin within a luxury industry largely dominated by famous European brands.

And as a proud Belgian (and with Belgium being the world's most celebrated chocolate-producing nation, with internationally known brands like Godiva and Côte d'Or), I must also highlight the outstanding work of a more boutique brand: Pierre Marcolini. Early on in his career, Pierre Marcolini differentiated himself as an 'haute couture' chocolatier. Elegantly nestled in its designer-styled packaging, Marcolini products combine some of the world's finest and rarest cocoa beans—from select plantations in Venezuela's seaside or state farms on the island of Java, Indonesia—with innovative flavours such as emerald-green pistachios from Iran. Take a mouthwatering bite, close your eyes and get ready to embark on a luxurious voyage for the connoisseur palate.

When I work with clients on their digital marketing, they usually tell me, 'We need to generate more revenue'. But very few understand their underlying objectives and what they need to do in order to make this happen. The success of your digital marketing strategy lies in knowing very clearly the type of consumers you are targeting. If you try to please everyone, you don't attract anyone. So no matter what project, I always spend time discussing with my clients the business niche that they are trying to serve.

Remember: defining your niche is especially important when marketing online because you generally only have a second or two to grab someone's attention. So you need to be really clear about the market you're trying to serve to develop initiatives that truly resonate with them. Instead of focusing on how to increase sales, beat the competition and dominate the market, ask yourself how you can build a luxury brand that people love to experience and talk about.

What's Your Brand Space?

Take some time now to define your ideal customer or client. Be as specific as you can, and try to look at your brand through your customers' world view. Think about those customers you've worked with who have really understood the value of what you were offering them.

Ask yourself:

- Is your brand or business specialising in a gender, age, ethnic group, occupation, income or family structure?
- Where are your customers located (geography)?
- What type of lifestyle do they live?
- What are they passionate about?
- What key problems or frustrations do they have?
- Why do they buy from you?
- What do they have in common?
- How digitally engaged are they and where?

Answering these types of questions can help you build a more complete picture of your niche market, meaning you can then start engaging with them more effectively (see the next section for more help with this).

Rules for Online Luxury Success for Niche Brands

To help you find your niche and engage with them effectively in the online space, I've come up with the following rules (or guidelines, at least!). Use the rules outlined in the following sections to boost your success.

DIGITAL SPARKLE

Luxury brands must experiment with digital innovations, without losing their brand's uniqueness and integrity.

Marry Something Old with Something New

Many luxury brands, especially heritage ones, are mainly family owned or managed from the top-down, which can sometimes result in them being slow to react to the changes brought by digital. And although maintaining brand consistency and integrity has proven effective in the past, digital and its effects on the cultural and behavioural habits of the affluent consumers require modern, more flexible and adaptable strategies.

Your approach needs to be about marrying traditions with cutting-edge media. So keep the stories about the people or family behind the brand, and the brand's heritage, but integrate these into your digital strategy.

Settle for Nothing Less than Bespoke Strategies

If you're working with an agency, don't just accept a basic 'cookie-cutter' type strategy. Luxury brands need to provide unique and customised online luxury experiences, so digital agencies that serve luxury need to innovate and customise for luxury beyond the best practices of mainstream brands. (See chapter 12 for more on working with an agency.)

Build a Digitally Empowered Team

Luxury CEOs and their senior management teams need to understand at least the fundamentals of digital and what it encompasses. Only then will they be able to make strategic and tactical decisions to lead their brands to innovation.

Provide a First-class Experience (and the Rest will Follow)

The web will amplify your reputation, for good or for bad. In an open and transparent online and offline world, controlling what people say about you is impossible. But you can certainly influence the conversations. All of the digital touchpoints you have at your disposal are capable of deteriorating the consumer's relationship with your luxury brand—from an email that cannot be viewed properly on mobile, to web pages that are too slow to load. Equally, all touchpoints are capable of enhancing customer engagement and building relationships. Focus on providing an extraordinary customer experience across the purchase journey.

Test, Learn, Refine—Again and Again

The only way to evolve in an organic online world is to experiment your way to success. You must foster continuous learning and improvement, and innovate and test until you find what works best for your business and your niche market.

Be Patient with Return on Investment

Building strong relationships and a strong presence online takes time. What's great about digital is that you can make informed decisions and innovate economically and intelligently. Building engaged customers takes time and you may not see a return on your investment immediately. You just need to give digital marketing an opportunity to prove itself.

Be Customer-centric

We no longer aspire to brands and what they represent—we want them to aspire to us. So a luxury brand has to demonstrate how it brings its luxury cachet to enhance our lifestyle, and then help us to reflect those luxury values to tell our own unique story. The new affluent consumers want products and services that dazzle their senses and touch their hearts. Again, this is where finding, and truly understanding, your niche market will pay off in developing your digital strategy.

Make the voice of your customer an integral part of the product and service development process.

First Does Not Necessarily Mean Best

Many luxury brands avoid looking at what the competition is doing because they believe that if they are not the first to do something, doing something similar is pointless. In other words, these brands believe there is no room for innovation.

But think about it. Google was not the first search engine, Facebook was not the first social media site and the iPhone was not the first smartphone. But they have all revolutionised their respective industries, by improving and re-evaluating a pre-existing concept. Look at where your niche market is—the sites your customers love and the platforms they're active on—and innovate from there.

Getting Immersive and Experiential with Digital

When discussing luxury digital marketing, the British luxury fashion house Burberry is widely recognised as a leading example of how to do it right. Indeed, digital is now part of the brand's DNA. Burberry has managed to successfully marry its prestigious fashion empire with the digital world, giving consumers the luxury products they truly desire in the fast, convenient manner they have grown accustomed to, and providing new ways for customers to interact with the brand.

Back in 2009, for example, Burberry launched Art of the Trench, a social networking site where users could share their trench looks from around the world. In 2010, Burberry launched Runway to Reality, a click-to-buy initiative where select VIP customers could stream runway shows live and order items directly from the catwalk, with the items then delivered within six weeks. At the time, this time frame was totally revolutionary in the industry.

Even today, Burberry is continually finding new ways to further innovate and integrate their physical and digital platforms to enhance the brand experience across all touchpoints. These strategies range from investments that leverage data and insight in the creation of increasingly personalised customer experiences, to more integrated, emotive storytelling across the online and offline worlds.

To take full advantage of customer data and analytics, Burberry uses initiatives such as Customer 360—an opt-in data-driven program that invites customers to digitally share their buying histories, purchase tendencies and shopping preferences. These customers' profiles can then be accessed through hand-held tablets by frontend staff, allowing them to better serve customers by anticipating their needs—for example, through making on-the-spot recommendations based on previous purchases or preferences, like suggesting a clutch bag to go with the dress a customer had bought on their previous stopover trip. Collecting such data also allows Burberry to further refine its marketing effectiveness by reallocating marketing spend more tactically.

Burberry has embraced a 'digital first' ethos so thoroughly it has invested deeply in digitally integrated brand experiences and multimedia-infused immersive retail initiatives. Its Regent Street flagship store in London, for example, features cutting edge on-screen technology, audio-visual simulated rain showers and smart radio-frequency identification (RFID) tags on clothes that turn into screens, displaying relevant content such as live runway feeds.

Even though Burberry is a huge, international luxury brand, its success comes from both truly adopting digital and truly knowing and engaging with its customers—something luxury brands of all sizes can do.

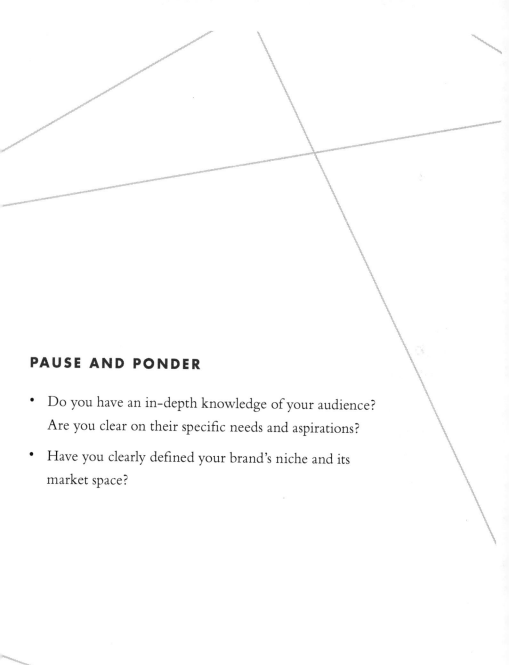

PAUSE AND PONDER

- Do you have an in-depth knowledge of your audience? Are you clear on their specific needs and aspirations?

- Have you clearly defined your brand's niche and its market space?

CHAPTER 7

Engaging Your Customers

GONE are the days of dull corporate messaging, and in this age of increasing digital noise, it is no longer enough to simply produce content—even if it's great content. Instead, you need to focus on creatively telling your authentic brand stories to your audience. And you need to use those stories to truly engage people and turn them into loyal customers—and vocal defenders of your brand. This chapter shows you how.

Articulating the Intangible: the Art of Telling Stories

Stories have always been part of our lives, right from when we first started to speak. No doubt you can easily remember the fairy tales of childhood—they made us cry, they made us laugh. They made us fear, and they made our palms sweat and our hearts race. They made us love. Years after, we still remember how these stories made us feel—how they stirred our emotions, awakened our senses and captured our imagination. Stories have always had the power to make an everlasting impression.

DIGITAL SPARKLE

Great storytelling is about addressing both the mind and the heart and creating personal, meaningful and memorable experiences worth coming back to.

In the luxury context in particular, where purchases are not a necessity and thus rely heavily on how a brand can make us feel, storytelling is paramount. Every brand has a unique story to tell, but luxury brands, with their heritage, focus on unique quality and bespoke craftsmanship, often have the richest stories to tell. So the content is there; what luxury brands need to focus on is telling their stories in a contemporary way that appeals to the new affluent consumers.

Luxury is all about selling a desired dream, a special feeling, a unique experience. And affluent consumers embrace brands that tell them truthful and meaningful stories—stories of heritage and tradition, stories of desire, stories of craftsmanship and beauty, stories about sustainability and other behind-the-scenes details. And digital has the potential to provide these stories and more, through immersing the luxury consumers in very innovative ways. In an increasingly crowded luxury marketplace, therefore, luxury brands are required to find the right balance between the intrinsic product features and the intangible values.

Luxury brands must focus on human needs and emotional triggers to create long-lasting relationships. Luxury brands must engage their consumers' emotions to drive a connection that leads not just to awareness, but also to brand advocacy and guardianship.

Luxury brand stories can focus on:

- *Brand history and heritage:* what's the foundational story behind your brand? Who founded it? What were the guiding principles? Where did the idea for your product or service come from?
- *Brand lifestyle and beliefs:* what values are most important to you? What are your brand's core beliefs, your passion and your reason for being? Young or old, all great brands and individuals stand for something—it's the starting point for every story.
- *Brand experience:* communicating the authentic experience of a brand is absolutely essential for luxury storytellers. Rather than simply telling consumers how to use products, tell the story

of how the brand can be experienced for self-affirmation and peer-affirmation.

- *Brand persona:* what sort of person does the brand represent and who is worthy of mingling with or owning the brand? These aspects are easily turned into stories.

Now that I've given you some of the basics behind good storytelling, use the following elements for help with mastering the art of storytelling.

Storytelling is Not (All) About You

Good storytelling involves a deep understanding of who your target audience is, so listen to what your audiences want to talk about and craft your storyline to cater to their demand and pulse. Find out what they think. You may be surprised.

Ask yourself:

- What do your customers truly want or need?
- How do they interact with your brand?
- What are they saying about your brand?
- How does your brand affect their lives?
- How much do they know about you?

Gaining these sorts of customer insights will ensure that your story isn't just great but also relevant to your audiences.

Incorporate Your Brand's DNA in Your Story

Focus on ideas that would inspire your target audiences. Compare your brand with key competitors and place your brand's DNA at the core of each narrative.

Find answers to the following:

- What are your brand's unique values?
- How do your customers describe your brand?
- Does your brand have an authentic story behind it that no other brand can use?
- What is the clear, consistent direction for your brand?
- What messages do other brands convey and how can yours be different?
- Where are you going, and where do you want your brand to be?

Solve Problems

Storytelling allows brands to show how their products or services can solve problems, subtly. Storytelling does not overwhelm your customers with the pure benefits or features that you offer, but rather illustrates these benefits quietly, allowing everyone to draw their own conclusions.

Tell a Great Story

As mentioned, we all love a great story, so craft a compelling one by merging your ideas with emotion and imagination. Add a soul to your story with characters and be colourful. One word of warning: using your imagination is great, but avoid making things up—like product benefits. You need to stay true to your brand, products or services, and industry.

How can you make your story distinctive? This exercise can help you piece together your message:

- Translate your brand's characteristics into keywords
- Sort the keywords and pick the ones that reflect your brand most
- Rank the selected keywords
- Formulate the message to describe your brand.

Remember: focus on things that inspire, entertain and eventually engage with your audiences.

Understand the Power of Emotions

Engage, entertain and excite, keeping in mind that emotion is at the heart of every story, in every age, in every context. Even in the digital age, we connect with stories on a human level, and we are seeking connections that are true, emotional and personal.

Creating a section on your website highlighting your customers' anecdotes or success stories, for example, is a great, personal way to boost your brand storytelling efforts.

Use Visual Storytelling

The brain processes visual information 60,000 times faster than text, so you need to have not only a clear narrative when telling your brand story, but also strong images to empower your approach. Combine the power of photos, illustrations, infographics, behind-the-scenes snapshots, text, audio, videos and animations to create a rich multi-sensory experience and help your audiences digest your message. Your approach should be all about enchanting people's daily lives.

Remember: Consistency, Consistency, Consistency

Being consistent doesn't mean that you can only post the same story over and over again. But your key messages should be consistent with your overall brand positioning. People should be able to easily associate your basic story with your brand. The brand position for Tiffany & Co., for example, is all about celebrating expressions of romance and the world's greatest love stories, and their storytelling always reflects this. Rolex, on the other hand, embodies excellence and innovation, and is a symbol of extraordinary achievements from The Championships at Wimbledon to the Formula One World Championship. Again, its storytelling consistently reinforces this.

Create Viral Proof

Digital is opening up a whole new era of opportunity, putting the power to create emotive content and share it widely in everyone's hands. Make your story irresistibly shareable. Integrate social media into your creative content to get real-time responses from your target audiences: embed social sharing buttons and proactively post your story on your social network channels to encourage more sharing and reach wider audiences.

Let Your Audience Tell Your Story

Taking things a step further, you can also engage your audiences on a deeper level in the story. Good user-generated content is known to create amazing levels of engagement and can become viral very quickly, so invite your audiences to be part of the story production process: ask for their feedback about a storyline and which character they would like to see. Ask them to vote on which song they want to hear within a video, or which scenario they prefer. Seeing their preferences come to life will increase user engagement enormously, and help create vocal brand advocates.

Use the Same Story on Different Channels

With so many engaging media at your disposal, your brand story should not only be communicating and engaging with your consumers through videos, blog posts or infographics, but also throughout your website, customer care lines, chat lines, mobile apps—the list goes on. So map all of your brand's touchpoints and ensure you're taking full advantage of each. You will then nurture the process of interest, purchase, repeat purchase and brand loyalty.

If you don't have enough resources, you can start with one medium first, and then evaluate, improve and expand from there. (See chapter 10 for more on measuring your digital success.)

Give Your Branded Content an ROI

Make sure your approach to storytelling is strategic and linked to real KPIs, and track your story's performance and engagement rate across the multiple channels that you use. The data will be a valuable reference to help you improve your future content marketing plan and make your next story more powerful.

Remember: storytelling has always been one of the best ways for luxury brands to make their customers desire them, and achieve a sense of life enhancement from them, and this remains the case in the digital age. So be ready to take your audiences through an unforgettable journey of your brand story.

Now that we've run through the 11 keys to crafting a powerful story and some of the kinds of stories you can explore, let's look at some examples of luxury brands that have led the way to amazing narratives in the luxury industry.

Luxury Storytellers: Combining Style and Substance

Louis Vuitton's 'L'Invitation au Voyage', a journey between fantasy, drama, dream and reality (and featuring David Bowie), is a great piece of storytelling that communicates both the brand's heritage and its continuing relevance. The key promise of the Louis Vuitton group is to represent the most refined qualities of Western *art de vivre* (art of living) internationally, and so Louis Vuitton uses this storytelling to effectively communicate its brand values and philosophies, while making sure to touch the consumer in an authentic and emotional fashion.

Chanel is another great example of how to establish a resonating relationship between the essence of a brand and the consumer's self-identity. When consumers buy Chanel they feel they are buying into a lifestyle of Parisian elegance, and with its 'Once Upon a Time' and 'Once and Forever' fascinating capsule video series, Chanel has linked into this idea and demonstrated brilliantly how to use storytelling to create an emotional value.

Three things in particular made the 'Once Upon a Time' video so positively received by affluent consumers:

- The video begins with 'Once upon a time... ' just like a traditional story read from a fairy tale book.
- The story has as a protagonist: Coco Chanel herself.

- The story has a powerful plot, telling the story of Coco Chanel, a woman with a complicated life out to change the face of fashion, dealing with realistic obstacles and eventually having the confidence and courage to challenge tradition and make the brand into one of the most admired brands in the world today.

This video can be found among other fascinating capsule videos on the Inside Chanel microsite, a visual ride inside Chanel's legacy and values.

Tiffany & Co. has also used great storytelling with its microsite 'What Makes Love True', through allowing people to share photos of their most romantic moments and memories. This was a great way for Tiffany & Co. to leverage user-generated content to tell their story in a way that feels truly authentic.

And in March 2012, Cartier unveiled 'L'Odyssée de Cartier', a fantasy video offering a unique moment of escape from Paris to the Great Wall of China, and beyond. Cartier has a strong sense of heritage and the brand never fails to highlight that aspect—whether through its position as a pioneer in the art of watchmaking or the panther that has been its icon since 1914. All these aspects were captured through the storytelling in this campaign.

Another luxury brand that masters the art of storytelling is Mont-blanc. Its website and social media platforms are peppered with great stories—stories of craftsmanship, stories of style, stories of heritage. For its iconic 'power pen', the Meisterstück—spotted in the hands of some of the most affluent decision-makers in the world (from Presidents Kennedy to Barack Obama) and the rich and famous—Montblanc has managed to position this writing instrument as a true lifetime companion. This is the pen that celebrates and documents important life milestones, such as graduations, marriages and career promotions. Through its microsite My Meisterstück, Montblanc also invites consumers to share their own personal stories.

I've used these examples from larger, more well-known brands to inspire you and because the power to their storytelling is easily recognisable. Again, even though these brands may have bigger budgets than you do, you can still use the same approaches to telling the unique story of your brand and engaging your customers.

PAUSE AND PONDER

- Do you know what your customers truly want and need so you can craft your storytelling to cater to their desires?

- What is your brand's unique DNA, and have you incorporated this into all your stories?

- Have you involved your audience in your story, allowing them to create content and building engagement on a deeper level?

- Have you combined everything your brand stands for and everything your audience looks for in a luxury brand into your storytelling? Have you included style and fantasy, communicating your brand's heritage, craftsmanship and quality?

CHAPTER 8

Building a Powerful Online Presence

LUXURY brands encounter many struggles and challenges in their digital journey, including a general tendency to focus on short-term gains as opposed to long-term digital investments. These common challenges, however, can be overcome with the right approach.

With consumers spending an increasing amount of time online, luxury brands must ensure a seamless journey towards brand discovery across all channels. This means you must give sufficient thought to defining a business roadmap that answers the following questions:

- What is your purpose?
- What are your guiding principles?

Answering these questions will then help you with implementing your digital strategy holistically across all touchpoints. In this chapter, I take you through some of the aspects involved with this, focusing on helping you build a powerful online presence through your website.

Refining Your Brand Website

Your website is the window to your brand's soul, and as the common first stop for most affluent consumers when they search for information about you brand, your website is at the core of your luxury brand's digital presence. Web design trends may come and go, but one thing will remain constant over time: the need for a first-class user experience. And while high-end brands need to strive to maintain an air of exclusivity that feels aspirational and not overly accessible, this exclusivity should not be maintained at the detriment of a great user experience.

Of course, luxury brands must ensure their online presence meets the same high-calibre service standards set in their brick-and-mortar stores. The in-store luxury experience is crafted with meticulous attention to detail and centered on fulfilling the every need of discerning customers, and luxury brands' online presence must mirror this thoughtfulness, finding the right balance between luxury design and great functionality.

Before looking in more detail at what makes a great website, however, let's look quickly at some of the common mistakes luxury websites make.

Understanding the Common Mistakes Made by Luxury Websites

The following sections outline what to avoid with your luxury website.

Slow Load Times

The time it takes for a page to load is a key element in any website user experience, with a lengthy page load time becoming an invitation for the visitor to click away. In fact, nearly half of online visitors expect a site to load in 2 seconds or less, and they tend to abandon a website that isn't loaded within 3 seconds (according to a study by Akamai, a leading content delivery network services provider specialising in speeding up delivery of content over the internet; this study was released several years ago, so it's likely that web users' expectations are even higher now).

Unfortunately, slow loading times appear to be a common theme among luxury websites, and often this poor performance is due to a lack of optimisation. But websites do not need to compromise on speed to accommodate better aesthetic design—and all the bells and whistles required to create a unique experience. Rich graphics and images can be used, but they should always be optimised to ensure great website performance.

Poor Readability

Readability is a crucial component of a website's usability. Yet, many luxury brands make design choices that are challenging from a user experience perspective, including:

- fancy font styles that may look pretty but are near impossible to decipher
- tiny font sizes that require magnifying glasses to view properly
- low contrast colour schemes that make reading very tiring to the eyes.

Remember: no matter what message you're trying to get across, nothing will get through if the content just isn't easily readable.

Intrusive Splash Page and Animations

How often have you gone onto a luxury website and been forced to watch an introduction while you were desperately trying to find the 'skip' button hidden in a small corner of the page? And how frustrating is it when you land on a splash page and have to make that extra click to access the content you actually care about?

Although splash pages are usually graphically rich, they are often completely unnecessary and can have harmful effects on website performances and search engine rankings. While some may argue that this is an integral part of the immersive luxury brand experience, you should leave it up to your users' discretion as to whether or not they view the splash screen promotions or videos.

Mystery Navigation

Up, down, left, right … Where am I? Where have I been? Where can I go next? Navigating through some luxury websites can be overwhelming. Visitors to your website want to access the information they came for in the most timely manner. Unfortunately, many luxury websites do not have a clear navigation path and do not incorporate site search.

Plus, many luxury brands fail to use the most relevant descriptive terms for their products and pages, and the ones that are most helpful to their target customer base. Instead, luxury brands use ambiguous names for web pages that do not clearly define what each page features.

Automatic Sound

Have you ever opened a website at the office, in the library or any other quiet public space and suddenly some loud music hits you in full swing. You can't immediately locate the mute button so you reflexively close the site to make it stop. Sound familiar?

Many luxury brands incorporate background music and videos that autoplay as soon as a visitor arrives on the site. Unfortunately, more often than not, these imposed sounds are intrusive and can be very irritating, especially when blaring out when you least expect it. It's important to always display a prominent audio control so that users can easily stop the music or change the volume in a hurry.

Not Optimised for Mobile Devices

The luxury shopper is more mobile than ever. Providing a seamless user experience across all devices is thus paramount if luxury brands want to reach consumers in all the moments that matter. Being optimised for mobile devices is no longer optional.

Not Optimised for Search Engines

The correct technical setup of a website is a key element of search engine optimisation (SEO). Simply put, SEO is a set of techniques that allows websites to rank on the top of the major search engines' organic (unpaid) results. In other words, SEO is all about finding ways to increase your site's appearance in search results. And today, being visible online is just as important as your visibility in the offline world.

Unfortunately, if luxury brands usually invest tremendous effort and resources into having outstanding boutiques in prime locations, they often ignore SEO best practices and, as a result, search engines are often unable to index all their pages. Luxury shoppers are indeed increasingly relying on Google searches and social networks to find products, engage with their favourite luxury brands wherever and whenever they want, and make their purchase. This means reliable online search results are essential and SEO is an untapped opportunity for luxury brands.

Looking at the Anatomy of a Great Luxury Website

So, now that we've looked at the common mistakes, what elements make up a luxury site?

There are many, but here are four of the most important:

- Mobile-friendliness
- Flawless design and attention to detail
- First-class user experience and usability
- Great copy

Making it Mobile-Friendly

With today's consumers constantly connected on a wide array of devices and screen sizes, savvy businesses know that it's absolutely essential to have a mobile-friendly or, more precisely, a multi-screen website if they want to reach consumers in all the moments that matter.

Building a successful responsive website for the multi-screen consumer requires five essential best practices. These are covered in the following sections.

Laying the Groundwork

Building a website for multiple devices starts with understanding your audience and mapping your customer's journey. Using web analytics (such as Google Analytics), identify your website goals, your source of traffic, your visitors' actions on the site and their various behaviours.

This insightful information will enable you to define the most used, and the most needed functionalities for your website, helping you answer the needs of both your customers and your business. For example, retailers may need to emphasise their store locators and provide an extensive product search.

Responsive Content

When designing a responsive website, thinking about your content before your design is important, because doing so means you are more likely to give your audience what they need and desire. Developing responsive content is about telling your story in a way that's valuable to your visitors in the multi-screen context in which they are interacting with your website.

Your customers want to easily get to the information or functionality they need, on whatever device they happen to be—don't expect your visitors to scroll endlessly to discover the content they're interested in, for example.

A simple structure for your site and content prioritisation are thus key aspects to a successful responsive website. Consider the following:

- Be concise and clear; hint and hook. Make your content easily scannable and 'snackable' by using short sentences, clear sub-headings and lots of bullet points.
- Craft key messages to ensure your message is heard. These messages should answer your customer's informational needs at

the top level, but your content should also allow further details to be found as they navigate down the page or onto additional pages.

• Provide the same core functionalities for your mobile users as you offer desktop users. This is now the expectation of mobile users. (See the following section for more on this area.)

• Ensure your calls-to-action aren't lost at the bottom of the page. You can highlight these by adding some logical breaks further up the page to reinforce and encourage these actions.

Mobile-first Design

With mobile fast becoming the primary mode of internet access, you should no longer consider mobile users as a secondary audience. Businesses need to think mobile-first and plan the website layout with mobile users in mind.

Simplicity and clear focal points are key when working on mobile-first design, and the following are the core features to designing responsively:

• *Touch-friendly buttons:* make sure buttons and links are large enough to tap with a thumb, and are placed far enough apart so that the correct button can be easily tapped.

• *Thumb-friendly navigation:* your site should be easy to navigate vertically with the swipe of a thumb. Make sure users are not forced to scroll horizontally to see the entire content as this makes for a bad user experience. Opting for a sticky menu (meaning the navigation bar stays at the top of the page when people scroll down) is also worth considering. And if your website has a complex, multi-level navigation, take some time to think of the best way to prioritise and structure your menu for your visitors to intuitively reach their destination. For help with this, I recommend you use the data from the Users Flow report in Google Analytics to reveal your most popular pages and understand how traffic flows around your site.

- *Clean typeface and viewer-friendly font size:* make your text easy to read without your users needing to pinch and zoom-in on the screen.
- *Click-to-call button:* make contact easily accessible, especially at drop-off points on the customer conversion journey.
- *Avoid mouse-overs:* on a desktop screen, mouse-overs might be a great way to uncover hidden content but hover effects do not work on mobile devices. Instead, opt for buttons that users can tap to display deeper menus.
- *Descriptive buttons:* label your buttons clearly so that customers know exactly where a click will take them.
- *No pop-ups:* these can be very irritating, especially on mobile sites.
- *Finger-friendly forms:* keep forms simple by breaking them down into simple steps and using a minimum number of input fields that customers can easily fill out without having to pinch and zoom.

Need for Speed

Smartphone users are impatient—they want and expect information to load quickly. No matter how cool your website is, if it doesn't load fast enough, visitors (and thus potential customers) will leave without a second thought. According to research by Google, 61 per cent of mobile users will quickly move onto another site if they have a bad mobile experience. And a slow loading page sure is a major frustration! Overall site speed is also a factor, with optimised speed typically boosting visitors' engagement, retention and conversion.

Your site speed can also affect your ranking on search engines—with Google striving to always offer the best user experience on all devices, page speed is also an important ranking factor on mobile search queries.

Test, Refine, Repeat

Last but not least, keep testing, analysing and optimising your site to debug any issues that might occur and to best meet the ever-evolving user viewing habits. (See chapter 10 for more on monitoring your digital success.)

Remember: multi-screen consumers call for a new approach to designing websites. This new approach requires a shift in mindset—from barely implementing a website that also works on mobiles to mobile-friendly (or mobile-first) design fundamentally encompassing the unique needs of mobile users and becoming an essential element of your marketing strategies.

Ensuring Flawless Design

For luxury brands in particular, controlling the visual brand identity is vital because this identity captures the brand's essence and the emotional values associated with it.

Luxury consumers are accustomed to shopping in exquisite boutiques and they have impeccable standards—and they hold your brand to these standards, especially across the many offline touchpoints. Colours, shapes and in-store displays play an important role in feeding your consumers' desire for your products and experiences. And now, offline and online experiences must fully align so as to mutually complement each other in the delivery of your brand's story.

DIGITAL SPARKLE

Translating the feeling of sophisticated elegance, timelessness and luxury to the online world starts with impeccable and tasteful design.

So it is crucial that your brand's website conveys that uniquely identifiable and high-end feel.

Everything from the colour palette to the placement of elements such as the logo, the graphics, the icons and the images should be meticulously thought out to create powerful stories that capture the imagination.

To ensure flawless design and a consistent brand message on your website, consider using the following:

- *Consistent and/or emotive colours:* you can use colours consistently to enhance your brand's signature and personality (for example, we expect to see some red for Ferrari, black for Chanel and orange for Hermès). The colour selection is also important because it can influence our emotions and create a powerful first impression online. Colours add beauty, meaning and context to your site, and are especially important in the digital era because consumers typically make up their mind in a matter of seconds—which is precisely why you need to select a colour palette that reinforces your brand's identity and clearly conveys the right message to your audience. For example, black is mostly used to convey a sleek, luxurious idea or market a high-end product (and is often used by many luxury sites as their main colour for this reason). You can use tools such as colour wheels to help you build up your palette, and then test, edit and experiment with your designs to choose what works best for your brand.
- *Clean and sleek interface, along with glossy digital videos and photography for elegant storytelling:* displaying visual elements in the right context is a crucial point that enhances the visual impact of your luxury brand's website. Ensure you use sleek, high-quality imagery when showing samples of your products. A luxury product must look worthy of its status, so ensure

you present the product in all its glory and allow customers to inspect all of its intricacies and craftsmanship.

- *Tasteful graphics (including drawings, sketches, charts and tables):* these can contribute to how much and how easily users recall your products, and are features and messages that can reinforce your brand's identity.

For an example of great design, have a look at the Rolex website. Through the site providing macro images of their watch components in high definition, Rolex consumers can be amazed by their precious details and precise internal mechanics. The images also give a certain proximity to the products, as if we could unveil all their secrets. Rolex uses its site to powerfully tell the story of its craftsmanship in a way it can't at a retailer location.

Think about how you could use your site to create the same sort of experience. Perhaps you can provide a 360-degree view of your products. Consumers want to be able to see close-ups of the materials and details about the products—such as the grain on a leather bag, the stitching of a suit or the delicate fluidity of a silk dress.

Of course, keep in mind that a luxurious website must be not only beautiful to look at but also functional, offering a great user experience.

Adding a First-class User Experience

Providing a first-class user experience (UX) focuses on having a deep understanding of users—their expectations, emotions, abilities and limitations. The focus is on understanding the intuitions and the connections a user feels when interacting with your digital interfaces, and on improving the quality of those interactions. The user experience you provide can be seen as a reflection of your online customer service, and about taking the time to get to the heart of what users are looking for (and what they didn't even know they wanted) to provide a pleasant, convenient and efficient online experience.

The user experience is important because of the following key areas:

- *Customer satisfaction:* the user experience on your website will play a critical role in attracting and maintaining your customer base. Your customers are your users, and these users will be satisfied if they have a positive experience on your website—one where their expectations are fulfilled. Most visitors decide within a matter of seconds whether to stay on your site or look for something better. If users find it easy, pleasant and natural to achieve a given task, your website will likely be used more often. Customer satisfaction is very much needed to keep your business healthy and growing.
- *Customer loyalty:* satisfied customers provide the foundation for customer loyalty, and a great user experience has the power to bring a customer back to your website. Happy visitors are more likely to purchase more from you and more often, and be vocal supporters of your brand. And more loyal customers mean less consumer education and marketing costs, especially

if these customers are acting as your brand advocates. Having this kind of customers should be your ultimate goal, and great UX helps achieve just that.

- *Efficiency:* with a faster and an easier-to-navigate site, users will more easily find what they are looking for (or, even better, buy more products) from a single visit to your site.
- *ROI and conversion rates:* all the effort and investment you put into your website will be rewarding once you achieve a great user experience—because a great user experience can result in an increased conversion rate and/or sales.
- *Brand touchpoints:* your business presence fitting with your customer desires increases your brand strength, which will make your business stand out from the competition.

Finding Your Website Sweet Spot

Inspired by the UX Honeycomb from Peter Morville, here are seven key elements a brand needs to focus on when creating a great user experience online:

1. *Purpose:* define innovative content and solutions that are useful for users. Remember: for something to be useful, it needs to have a practical purpose. The goal is to entice visitors to complete a desired action.

2. *Usability:* good usability means that the product meets the needs and goals of the users so that they can complete the task at hand quickly and easily. Ease of use (interface-centered methods and human–computer interaction) is vital, but keep in mind that only having a user-friendly interface is insufficient.

3. *Desirability:* create emotion and desire for your brand in your design with the power and value of image, identity, brand and other elements. A great user interface will create a welcoming tone.

4. *Searchability:* strive to design navigable websites and locatable objects, so users can easily find what they need.

5. *Accessibility:* content must be easily accessible (user-friendly, intuitive and adaptable) for all users. Consider building your website in a way that people with disabilities can still access the information, and ensure that your site is compatible with the different devices, operating systems and browsers that your visitors are using.

6. *Credibility:* the design of your website should reinforce the credibility of your brand. Design elements should influence and build users' trust.

7. *Value:* at the core of UX is ensuring that users find value in what you are providing to them. Ultimately, your site must improve customer satisfaction.

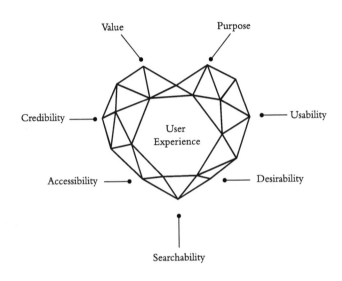

WEBSITE SWEET SPOT

Value

Purpose

Credibility

User
Experience

Usability

Accessibility

Desirability

Searchability

Creating Great Copy

I cover the power of great storytelling in chapter 7, and similar ideas extend to all of the copy on your website. Content marketing is about creating and publishing relevant and valuable content (articles, infographics, ebooks, whitepapers, videos, webinars, podcasts, e-newsletters, and many more) to attract and retain a clearly defined audience, and sharing this content across multiple online channels.

In a nutshell, content marketing promotes your business via relevant content that engages potential customers. Your objective? To drive profitable customer actions.

The following sections outline some essentials when creating great copy for your website.

Write for Your Target Audience

Knowing your target or niche audience is fundamental to creating (and curating) highly relevant content, because this knowledge helps you determine what message will resonate with them. Start by analysing your products or services, your unique selling points and current customer base. Think about your niche market and what your market comes to you (and only you) for. Concentrate on your primary target group first.

Research Your Keywords

Note down what terms best describe your products or services and analyse what keywords currently drive visitors to your website with Google Analytics. Also brainstorm what keywords you think your prospects would likely type into a search engine to find your business and your competitors. Compare your list with the actual keyword statistics, such as search volumes and trends, and competition levels, using a tool such as Google AdWords Keyword Planner.

You can then produce a list of keywords you want to be found for, and use this list of specific keywords to create related content to meet your audience's needs.

One word of caution, however: do not pepper your content with all your selected keywords. Google penalises sites with promotional content that typically includes keyword stuffing. More importantly, this usually creates bad writing (the opposite of engaging content) and users will quickly realise this. Instead, create good content that's worth engaging with. If your audience finds your content valuable and worth sharing, so will search engines.

Develop a Content Calendar

Don't just write a list of topics and arbitrarily publish them. Create an editorial calendar—that is, a visualisation of your content publishing —and make sure your content is always relevant to your readers and to your brand, and is timely and unique. New, informative and targeted topics are valued by Google and positively influence your ranking. Think about which events and dates resonate with your audience, and tailor your content and publishing schedule around these.

Quality Wins over Quantity

Publish only valuable, memorable and entertaining information to build awareness, trust and a positive online reputation for your business. Strive to become the content authority and the 'go-to' source in your own domain space, with content that satisfies your audience's needs and naturally places your site on the top of search results.

Link Your Posts Internally

Add internal links within your content to the relevant information, product or service on your site (for example, previous blog posts) to generate more inbound traffic and boost your position on search results.

Distribute Your Content

Content distribution is a key SEO activity that helps to increase your ranking in search results. Include social media sharing buttons on your site and proactively connect with online influencers such as bloggers and editors within your industry to help ensure your content is distributed to a broader (though still relevant) audience across the web.

Measure Your Content Performances

Measure the performance of your content marketing with trackable KPIs in Google Analytics. Analyse your organic search ranking for top keywords, your reach (unique visits and geography of visitors), engagement (number of pageviews, bounce rate and time spent on page), number of inbound links, amount of referred traffic from key social media networks, social shares and bookmarks.

Based on these valuable metrics, make corrections and continuously enhance your content. (See chapter 10 for more on analytics and measuring your success.)

Be Found, Be Heard

Plan your content marketing initiatives ahead of time, evaluate and iterate continuously, and strongly grow your content. An integrated approach to content marketing and search engine optimisation is the sure winner.

DIGITAL SPARKLE

This is a marathon, not a sprint. Content marketing is a long-term commitment, and seeing the results of your hard work and the impact this has had on your business may take months.

At times, you'll lack motivation and want to give up. Many people will quit. But you won't. Stay focused and you will succeed. Keep creating fresh, engaging content and you will ultimately draw your audience closer.

PAUSE AND PONDER

- What behaviours, actions and emotions do you want to invoke through your website? Have you ensured this forms the foundation of your website design?

- Is your site guilty of any of the common errors, such as slow load times, poor readability or mystery navigation?

- Are you truly mobile-friendly? Have you included 'snackable' text with features such as touch-friendly buttons and thumb-friendly navigation?

- Is your design flawless, with high-quality imagery, consistent colours and a clean interface?

- Are you providing a first-class user experience, with great, timely content that boosts your search engine rankings?

CHAPTER 9

Moving from Control to Conversations with Social Media

FOR generations, luxury brands have focused their communications in key channels that allowed them to fully control their brand's messages. But this focus has meant luxury brands have mostly remained on the sidelines of the widening forms of open and transparent two-way communication. The challenge for many luxury brands now is that they can no longer control their brand's message and what's being said about their brands in the way they traditionally used to, because consumers now have this control. To succeed in social media, luxury brands must be ready to participate in two-way conversations.

Social media, by its very nature of openness across many media, seems to be at odds with what luxury traditionally stands for, such as exclusivity and prestige. This perceived disconnection has generally led to only cautious adoption of social media by luxury brands. Some luxury brands even think their clientele would likely not be on social media. They couldn't be more wrong. Of course they are on social media. Posting. Commenting. Reviewing. Rating. The new affluent consumers love to share their first-class experiences—whether these are an exotic vacation, a luxury spa experience or their latest luxury fashion pieces from the runway—with their social networks and beyond.

Social media has democratised content creation and given all the opportunity to publicise and share opinions about brands—and these opinions can spread across the internet in a matter of seconds. Social media puts the brands in the centre of user-powered discussions.

In more recent years, more and more luxury brands are slowly embracing social platforms and succeeding. When managed properly, social media allows luxury brands to assert their unique position, deeply connect with their audiences, and further their brand equity. Plus, social media can actually help maintain a sense of desirability by opening up your brand to aspirational customers and sharing rich stories and imparting a glimpse of the luxury lifestyle. In this chapter, I take you through ways to take advantage of social media with your brand.

Participating in the Conversation

The era of the autocratic, one-sided broadcast model of communication is far gone. Today's customers don't want to be sold a product or service—they want to build a relationship with someone who understands their needs. People expect ongoing, useful information that they need or want to help make their lives better, simpler or more fulfilling. People want real dialogues, and customers are dictating how and where they want to receive information. Google once mentioned that *WWW* now stands for what I *w*ant, *w*hen I want, *w*here I want it. We indeed live in the culture of 'now', of real-time gratification.

DIGITAL SPARKLE

Social media gives affluent consumers a voice in the conversations about your brand, and a sense of belonging and validation.

Today's luxury shoppers no longer purely trust what a brand says about itself. The affluent consumers also look to peer reviews and seek advice from their social networks when shaping their opinion of a brand.

This means a fear of participation in the social discussions does not protect luxury brands. The conversations are already taking place.

Think about the number of luxury brand social media pages that were not created by 'official' representatives of the brands. Consumers will talk about your luxury brand whether you like it or not, so you being involved in this conversation, and engaging with your market by inspiring and shaping the conversation, is a much better option. By understanding what your most passionate followers and customers value most, including how they want to be serviced and how your luxury brand fits into their lives, you can bond with them more strongly than ever before and engage in much richer conversations.

As I discuss in chapter 7, engaging with your customers is now a necessity for your luxury brand to grow, and doing so helps you to know more about your customers' needs and thus to anticipate their desires. Added to this, an active presence on social networks means an active and ongoing presence of your brand in customers' minds.

The best way to minimise the risk to damaging your brand on social media is to stay true to your brand's values and principles—in other words, to be authentic. Remember that you are communicating with people. People with feelings and thoughts. So listening to them and hearing what they have to say on how to make your business better is important. The only things you need to control are your business values and ethics, your offerings, your business model and the customer experience that you choose to deliver. Social media amplifies your reputation, good or bad, so make sure you stay true to your brand's core values and offer extraordinary experiences.

You can create frameworks or moments for participation to empower your customers to shape your story together with you, focusing on incentivising high-quality user-generated content (UGC)—content created and provided by your audience—in defined contexts. For example, you could use a hashtag (#) campaign, create social media contests or ask for comments on news articles. Fashion designer Marc Jacobs brilliantly involved his audience when he asked for social media submissions for potential models to be the brand's next fresh face for their advertising campaign, inviting digital savvy fashionistas to post their selfies to Instagram or Twitter with the hashtag #CastMeMarc.

Social media can also help luxury brands in their fight against counterfeits by educating consumers on how to distinguish genuine products from counterfeits and by identifying, in real time, any mention of their name and thus limiting the spread of fraudulent products.

As highlighted by NetBase in one of its recent reports, understanding consumer sentiment (how consumers perceive your brand) is essential to a luxury brand's success. You must also evaluate the intensity of emotion (brand passion) behind that sentiment. Are you winning the hearts of your customers? A key way to evaluate this is through keeping your finger on the pulse of social media.

Successfully Using Social Media

Let's look at some examples of how luxury brands are successfully using social media. Burberry is one of the early adopters of social media in the luxury sector, and remains quick to go wherever its customers are. From the unveiling of its collections on Twitter to live streams directly from the runway on YouTube, Burberry highly values connecting with its community, and has created accounts on most mainstream social networks. Following on from their success in social media, Burberry is now dedicating a substantial part of its budget to digital marketing.

In a more discreet (perhaps conservative) way, Chanel is also often mentioned as a top performer on social media. From its aspirational portfolio of elegance and beauty on Instagram, to its Twitter feed dotted with quotes from Coco Chanel and updates about Chanel collections, its social media approach reinforces and builds on its established brand. On its YouTube channel (tidily featuring thematic playlists), Chanel shares videos from photo campaigns and fashion shows, as well as 'making of' and other brand stories that transport viewers into the sophisticated world of Chanel.

Luxury fashion designer Victoria Beckham also knows how to fully leverage social media, engaging her global followers through both personal and brand messaging across multiple platforms. From sneak peeks to exclusive photos, videos, behind-the-scenes and other aspirational, dream-inducing content, she invites people into the Victoria Beckham world.

Another example is Marysia, an emerging high-fashion swimwear brand that nicely leverages their Instagram content to drive sales. The 'Shop Instagram' menu tab on their website lets customers simply click on the image and purchase the featured item online.

Marysia delivers a full experience on Instagram: their posts feature beach shots, healthy food, and inspirational moments for the brand (mentioning when they were featured in the media, or when their pieces were spotted on a celebrity).

When promoting your brand on social media, think about how your products or services fit into a certain lifestyle.

Creating a Sophisticated Social Media Presence

Luxury brands absolutely should embrace social media as part of their digital marketing strategy. There is no doubt about that. And luxury brands need to be fully committed to this strategy, and devote the resources (human and financial) to creating and maintaining a powerful social media presence in line with their brand status. So the real question centres on how to create a sophisticated social media presence that maintains your exclusive brand image and distinguishes your brand from more 'mainstream' brands.

Indeed, people often ask me if a difference exists in the way luxury brands should use social media compared to mass brands. My answer is yes and no. Let me explain…

While luxury brands are ultimately different from mainstream brands and thus should behave accordingly online, the same core rules still apply: every brand should offer a great customer experience that adequately meets the needs of its target audience. However, for luxury brands in particular, consumers' expectations are usually higher. A luxury brand cannot afford to be average. So I always advise brands to choose their platforms carefully. It is better to be excellent in a couple of select platforms rather than have an extensive range of poorly managed channels. Belgian luxury leather brand Delvaux, for example, concentrates on three social media channels only (Instagram, Twitter and Pinterest).

DIGITAL SPARKLE

Social media should be about building, nurturing and maintaining deeper connections and long-lasting relationships with affluent customers.

To develop your social media strategy, you need to firstly identify the essential qualities that define your luxury brand, secondly translate those values and quality of experience into relevant content, and finally deliver this content to your audience(s). So how best to do this? The following section explains all.

Getting Social Luxury Right—Best Practices

Social media needs to be considered as an integral part of your brand's overall marketing strategy. To help you with this, here are some key principles for luxury brands to retaining their cachet when using social media:

- *Create a well-researched and cohesive strategy:*
  - Plan strong social experiences through research, resources and commitment.
  - Define your core ethos. Every brand has an ethos that can be the centrepiece of its messaging in social media, whether this ethos is impeccable customer service or a commitment to innovation. Define your ethos and be consistent.
  - Only engage in social media after you fully understand who you are (values), where you come from (story) and where you are going (vision).
  - Ensure your online presence is a smooth extension of your overall marketing efforts, through staying consistent and true to your core brand values.
  - Choose the right social networks for your brand carefully. Take some time to research which social platforms make sense for your brand and offer the best fit for your goals. Don't be shallow in many social media platforms; be excellent in the relevant ones by allocating resources efficiently as opposed to spreading them thinly.

The suitability of social media channels should be decided according to the brand's objectives and brand personality, and where your audience is.

- Understand your target audience, their needs and motivations, and tailor your strategy to them. Social media provides valuable insights into the tastes, behaviours, wants and pain points of your consumers.
- Align your social media strategy with cultural events that complement your brand.
- Set clear objectives, benchmarks and metrics for all social initiatives.
- Set rules and guidelines before engaging in social media.

• *Create and curate high-quality content:*
- Develop original and engaging content that is relevant to your affluent consumers and deliver it in a timely fashion.
- Contextualise your content according to the context of each platform. Consider how your affluent audiences use the various social networks. For example, Twitter can be used for building and sustaining excitement around live events and news, Snapchat to present early glimpses of new collections and other behind-the-scenes actions, and Instagram as an inspiring diary to engage with and influence people.
- Promote a luxury lifestyle around your brand rather than solely focusing on product features, through providing

your community with frequent content around art, culture, fashion and travel (as long as this content is on brand).
  - Define your content through understanding what draws your brand loyalists, and expand on it.
- *Listen to the conversations and respond:*
  - Monitor all social conversations (including the latest news, sensitive topics and opinions) and be ready to react quickly and efficiently to maintain your valuable brand reputation.
  - Outline response times. When it comes to social media—and, in particular, when relating to customer relationship management—people expect a response 24/7. Be clear on how and when they will get a response.
- *Engage through discussions and interactions:* social media is all about involvement, participation, collaboration and sharing. Social media campaigns involving contests, live streaming, and behind-the-scenes insights draw customers into the world of the brand, encouraging a more authentic connection.
- *Create a brand world that strengthens your emotional bond with customers:* translate your unique traits and brand qualities to all the social media channels you're focusing on.
- *Craft unified high-quality visuals across channels:* this does not mean you need to use the same imagery across all social platforms, but you should have a clear theme running across all. Create a similar look and feel across these platforms to give your brand a unified and easily identifiable presence. Also take

the time to discuss the kind of visual impact and values you
want to communicate, and then carefully craft high-resolution
visuals that will resonate with your audience. Keep in mind
the following:

- Use high-quality videos and images
- Match the aesthetics and quality of your visuals with your
  brand, and ensure they are distinctive and flawless.

- *Grant exclusive access to behind-the-scenes:* leverage social media to
  share content about your awards ceremonies, collection debuts
  and more. A sneak peek at things to come can also drive a lot
  of anticipation and interest.

- *Know your consumers:* understand what they are talking about,
  what they like or dislike and where they share or search for
  information (including trending topics and the themes of
  conversations). Build this into your social media content
  calendar.

- *Know who your VIP influencers are and build rapport with them:*
  see the section 'Leveraging Digital Influencers', later in this
  chapter, for more on this.

- *Know more about new trends in your category and track competitors:*
  assess how different social channels are working for you
  and your competitors, and then formulate actions for
  improvements.

- *Build a strong sense of community and affinity with timely posts:*
  define the right frequency of social posts to stay front-of-mind

among high-value consumers while making them feel they are true luxury insiders, aware of the latest announcements and updates.

Remembering Your Responsibilities

Being social comes with responsibilities. Once you've entered the social realm, keep in mind these social media essential traits:

- *Be active:* continually update your profiles, and keep up with discussions and interactions with consumers.
- *Be disciplined:* only embark in a new social channel if you are committed to maintaining it. An anaemic social media presence reflects badly on a luxury brand.
- *Be relevant:* publish and share interesting topics and content that bring value to your audience.
- *Be authentic:* publishing and sharing content that is true to your brand's story and identity is the cornerstone of brand loyalty.
- *Be consistent:* stay true to your brand voice.

Leveraging Digital Influencers

The success of a brand's digital marketing campaign hinges on its ability to build trust online. True influence is no longer just about celebrity product endorsements and sponsored partnerships in film, television and print, mainly because simple paid sponsorships from celebrities and other famous people don't feel authentic anymore.

The digital revolution has led to the emergence of a new type of influencer, with consumers now looking to the opinions and experiences of everyday people to guide their purchase decisions. Building your brand's reputation is now about genuine, personal recommendations from believable and authentic digital personalities and social media stars. These digital influencers carefully curate fan bases with specific characteristics, giving luxury brands the opportunity to reach very targeted audiences.

Choosing the Right Influencers for Your Brand

Luxury brands can work with digital influencers in a number of ways:

- *Sponsored reviews and advertorials:* in this situation, the influencer creates an original piece of content centered around the brand or product.
- *Product placement:* here the influencer shows or mentions a specific product in his/her content.
- *Influencer appearance:* the influencer is invited to a branded event and shares content about the experience online.
- *Brand ambassador:* here the influencer advocates for the brand or product across all available channels.
- *Testimonials and endorsements:* the influencer appears in brand-owned content.
- *Affiliate marketing:* the influencer leads consumers to purchase featured products in photos and posts through affiliate links.

Clearly, you want a digital influencer with integrity—someone who you connect with and who is respected by your niche market. So you should always start by researching the needs and interests of your target audience to determine which influencer will be the best fit for your brand. Keep in mind the following:

- *Look beyond the number of followers:* do not choose influencers simply based on the size of their follower base, because having a large network does not mean they are very engaged with their readers (or their readers are engaged with them). This large audience also may not fit with your target, niche market. You want those influencers who have many engaged fans— fans who share their content, and comment and mention them on multiple social media platforms.
- *Select personalities who are in line with your brand positioning:* the influencer you choose should reflect your values, and have the right demographic profile of followers. Confirm that their tone of voice, visual aesthetics and taste are a perfect match for your brand.
- *Measure, optimise and iterate:* remember that this is about building long-term and personal relationships.

PAUSE AND PONDER

- Are you trying to control the conversations about your brand, or are you always encouraging more participation from your audience?

- Do you have a well-researched and cohesive social media strategy? Are you ensuring you remain active, relevant, authentic and consistent?

- How are you taking advantage of digital influencers in your market?

CHAPTER 10

Intelligence— Measuring Digital Success

THE digital bandwagon is easy to jump on. The difficulty lies in effectively driving it for maximum brand impact and growth. And a key part of proving the value and return on digital marketing investments is measuring the performance, results and outcomes of digital campaigns. However, this measurement is often neglected. You can't improve what you don't measure but, as Albert Einstein was reportedly fond of quoting, 'Not everything that counts can be counted and not everything that can be counted counts.' (William Bruce Cameron is said to have coined the adage.)

So, when measuring your digital success, you first need to work out what needs to be counted. With the enormous amount of data available and a rapidly changing business landscape, you must make data analysis a core element of your digital strategy. But which data? In this chapter, I take you through how to measure the performance of your digital strategy, and what measurements to focus on.

Understanding the Value in Measuring Performance

Albert Einstein is also reported to have said, 'Insanity is doing the same thing over and over again and expecting different results'. Although Einstein is disputed as the source of this quote, the sentiment is totally right. And in the digital context the sentiment is even more important—you continually need to be tracking, testing and refining, over and over again.

Measuring marketing effectiveness enables you to understand your marketing performance and thus provides the possibility to evaluate, learn and identify opportunities to improve your ROI. But when thinking of ROI, remember that you need to go beyond strictly financial terms, and consider the effect on long-term goals and brand awareness.

Digital media also provides a backchannel for data—data that can help you understand how your customers interact with your products or services, and help you measure the effectiveness of your digital strategies with increasing accuracy. Data on clicks, views, engagement, location, time of day and other powerful metrics can provide an insanely high level of insightful information about your customers' behaviours and preferences.

Done thoroughly and thoughtfully, measuring your digital efforts not only enables you to report on how well (or badly) you're doing, but also helps you make substantial progress moving forward and get budget buy-in from the rest of your organisation.

DIGITAL SPARKLE

Tracking and monitoring your performances provides the insight needed to make smart decisions and develop informed strategies in the future.

Importantly, business owners and marketers alike need to identify which metrics can be influential for business growth and revenue generation. Instead of spending time analysing actionable metrics that matter most for their business and really have an impact on the bottom line, too often marketers focus solely on 'vanity' metrics— obvious numbers or stats like the number of followers on social media channels, raw pageviews, or numbers of downloads. This can lead to shortsighted decision-making, so don't fall into this common pitfall. You've got to dig deeper. Whenever you start tracking a metric, ask yourself if the data gained from this metric helps you take action and make informed decisions.

I don't mean you should pay no attention to vanity metrics, but I do recommend that you also include more valuable metrics that provide more depth and fully demonstrate the value of your marketing and business efforts, analysing not only where the company is succeeding but also its specific areas of improvement. For example, instead of concentrating purely on your numbers of fans on Twitter, Facebook or Instagram, go beyond and analyse *who* you are reaching—analyse your active users, your key influencers, and your potential and existing customers. Another example of actionable metrics would be the open rates for two email subject lines in A/B testing. Based on accurate data, the results can pinpoint exactly which format version to choose for your next campaigns.

When defining metrics, I always tell my clients they should ensure they are what I refer to as SMART—that is:

- *Strategic:* start with the goals, objectives or outcomes you want to achieve. Good metrics embody strategic objectives and help assess and monitor whether or not you are on track to meet your company's particular long-term goals.
- *Manageable:* don't get lost in complex data. What is most important is what you do with your collected data.

Good metrics must always trigger concrete action based on your findings.

- *Accurate:* make sure the data are coming from credible sources, and that you are reliably interpreting the data. This is crucial to ensure buy-in at all levels of the organisation.
- *Relevant:* go beyond raw numbers. It is important to take the context into consideration when it comes to analysing data; they must be relevant to your business goals.
- *Timely:* good metrics must be periodically reviewed and revised to remain in line with your business goals as your business evolves over time. To improve your outcomes, make sure you track how today's data compare to prior time periods. Chart and watch the trends.

DIGITAL SPARKLE

Metrics are just a means to a bigger end: always connect your analytics to your goals.

As the digital ecosystem becomes more complex, understanding how all the elements are contributing to your overall business success, and what's working and not working, is vitally important. In this fast-moving environment, you need to be able to make changes quickly.

The beauty of digital is that data can be captured and consolidated almost in real time. But as online and offline marketing become more intertwined, the challenge is to understand the results of your integrated marketing efforts. Calculating your exact ROI can also be difficult, but the data you will be able to produce are well worth your efforts.

Unfortunately, I can't give you a simple, one-size-fits-all template, because the key areas of assessment will vary slightly based on your industry and product or service. In the following sections, however, I share a few pointers to assist you in measuring your digital marketing success and in knowing what measurements are the most relevant to your business.

How to Measure

Here I outline a step-by-step framework for measuring the power of your digital strategy. Note that the steps take you right from the initial concept of a campaign. This is because measuring your success shouldn't only commence once a campaign is in place and has been running for a while, but should form the basic framework behind the whole campaign.

Step 1: Identify Your Brand Goals

Define what success means for your business. Why are you doing what you are doing? What do you want to achieve through being online and through your particular campaigns? Having clear objectives is vital to delivering a significant return on your digital investments. Make sure your objectives are clear, executable, and valuable to your company (think both short term and long term).

Step 2: Establish Campaign Goals

Now that you have defined your goals on a macro level, you need to develop specific campaign goals. This is critical to determining which campaigns are effective and thus shaping your future efforts.

Typically, two main types of digital campaigns are used: branding and direct response campaigns.

At the very minimum, you should use Google Analytics and set up goals so you can track whether or not visitors to your site are taking the desired actions you want them to take when initiating these campaigns.

For example, say you want to track website conversion goals. In this overall goal, you'd track whether customers:

- Completed a checkout on an ecommerce site
- Filled out a contact form
- Signed up to newsletter
- Downloaded a PDF file
- Spent time on important web pages
- Engaged in social interaction (share/like/follow)
- Viewed a video

Tracking customers engaging in any (or all) of these activities would show that your strategies are creating the desired actions.

Step 3: Determine Your Metrics and KPIs

The key performance indicators (KPIs) of a campaign are the metrics that help you understand how you are doing against your objectives. Your metrics should be effective and meaningful and be tied to your business goals. Of course, you could spend days and weeks laying out numerous metrics in colour-coded spreadsheets. But just because you can measure something, doesn't mean you should. By identifying objectives and establishing clear goals and KPIs upfront, you can set realistic benchmarks, manage expectations and measure metrics that matter for your business.

KPI development is no easy task, especially considering that the digital ecosystem is getting more complex. When defining your KPIs it is thus important to understand both how elements are performing individually and in unison. This information will allow you to better optimise your strategy moving forward.

Although KPIs are customisable, I usually would categorise KPIs into four main categories, as follows:

- *Reach and acquire:* are you being seen? Are you visible to your audience and potential audience? How successful is your acquisition across earned, owned and paid media? Have you identified the channels that are bringing in your highest-value customers? How much does it cost you to get a new customer?

- *Onboard and engage:* are customers enjoying their experience with your brand? Are your online communities interacting with your content? Are you giving them a consistent experience, across all touchpoints?
- *Optimise and grow:* are you regularly optimising your marketing activities? Do you know how well your business is doing?
- *Nurture and retain:* have some of your new customers made a second purchase? What is the total value of each customer?

For more information on this, see the section 'What to measure', later in this chapter.

Step 4: Identify the Targets

Targets are the numerical values you set as indicators of success or failure. To define your targets use historical performance (that is, how you did previously; you can use averages or assumptions if your brand is new) or benchmarks against competitors. The process is iterative, and the more experience you have, the better you'll get at setting appropriate targets.

Step 5: Monitor and Execute Real-time Improvements

Once you've identified your KPIs and targets, you can track the performance of your campaigns and make adjustments and changes to your campaigns if required. Make sure you get sufficient data before you make amendments. Again, however, you can quickly feel like you're drowning in data. Here's what to focus on:

- *Track social mentions:* as part of brand-building online, social mentions (including likes and shares) are critical towards determining the success or failure of digital initiatives. Actively monitor what people say about your brand online by running regular keyword searches.
- *Analyse data and establish preliminary benchmarks:* look at data collected through multiple sources, and use your own data or that from competitors or your industry-level to set benchmarks. Analyse past business performance data (using 12 months' worth of data is ideal).
- *Build your scorecard:* a scorecard is a centralised, easily understood dashboard view of your digital marketing efforts. It contains your KPI metrics and measures progress towards your stated strategic goals in a timely manner.
- *Track your key metrics on a weekly basis:* test a variety of approaches to see which ones actually work best.
- *Turn insight into action:* interpret the metrics and take action. Statistics require interpretation to uncover meaningful intelligence, actionable insights and areas for improvement, and provide a big picture view on how digital impacts your overall business. Remember: the ultimate purpose of marketing metrics is to drive better decision-making.

- *Think beyond:* more than just keeping up with digital's evolution, use metrics to anticipate what's coming next and be more proactive in your campaign planning.
- *Don't focus solely on short-term data such as views, clicks, likes, downloads:* focusing all your energy on short-term data will lead to short-term strategies. What's more important is how those results can help you achieve your broader vision.

Those who can see the intrinsic value in investing the time, resources and effort into continually monitoring and measuring their digital initiatives will be the ones to ultimately profit from the very real business benefits digital can deliver.

Better measurement can improve campaign effectiveness and, most importantly, ensure a better return on investment for your overall marketing.

What to Measure

In November 2014, Google published its *Measuring What Matters Most* guide for marketers, arguing that through understanding and measuring what matters most, businesses and brands can focus on their best customers and the critical moments in their journey, and so improve marketing outcomes. I wanted to share my key takeaways from this guide, because they can help lay your measurement foundation.

The Right Metrics

Stop measuring everything possible and, instead, identify clear metrics before launching a campaign. With advances in analytics, it's possible to better align your metrics with your core business goals. Focus on your true business objectives and make sure your KPIs are in line with the real problems that you're trying to solve. Don't let organisational silos stop you from measuring what matters most.

Your Most Valuable Customers

Understand *who* your customers are, not just their transactions. Measure long-term customer value instead of pure revenue, and look at which channels bring you your best customers. You'll develop stronger, more profitable relationships and avoid wasting money and effort on customers who cost more than they're worth.

Your Valuable Touchpoints

Understand what your customer journey looks like and identify the role of each touchpoint. Think holistically about your marketing. Attribute credit to the various marketing touchpoints to uncover insights and opportunities that will help you invest more wisely and better connect with your customers.

The Incremental Impact of Your Marketing Spend

Identify vital channels and new opportunities across all devices—and then experiment to estimate the potential performance and value of your efforts (and stop what's not working). Make experimentation a regular part of your marketing cycles: keep testing and keep improving.

PAUSE AND PONDER

- What metrics are you tracking right now that you need to stop? Which metrics aren't you tracking that you should start focusing on?

- How much do you really know about your most valuable customers? Do you know how to acquire more of them?

- What does your customer journey look like for your business? Do you know your most valuable touchpoints?

- Do you know the incremental value of each of your media investments?

CHAPTER 11

Lean, Nimble
and Agile

WITH digital marketing evolving at an ever-increasing pace, you must have the nimbleness to respond to changing technologies and the ability to evolve in real time. At a micro level, you can use this agility to capitalise on a trend, a popular hashtag or any other newsworthy event at a moment's notice.

As an SME or niche luxury brand, you're perfectly placed to be lean, nimble and agile among some of your bigger competitors. In this chapter, I show you how to use this to your advantage.

Knowing When to Assess and How to Iterate

In digital, you need to evaluate and assess everything that you do, and to do so continually, as I emphasise throughout this book. Measuring your digital marketing efforts continually will help you identify what works and what does not work well for you, in turn helping you manage your budget more effectively. More than this, to be successful in your campaigns you need to constantly innovate, learn, improve and refine throughout the process. You need to be able to identify problems and react quickly.

At the very minimum you should assess your performances prior to embarking on a new project, during the course of the implementation and after the completion. Too often, luxury marketers lose their momentum once their project is live. But sustainable success greatly depends on how well you manage and optimise your projects and strategies in the long run. Remember: digital is not a sprint, it's a marathon.

And this might seem like an obvious statement, but when it comes to luxury, reputation and customer satisfaction are essential elements. The purpose of your brand is to satisfy (actually exceed) the luxury consumers' individual needs and expectations.

Luxury brands have created out-of-the-ordinary experiences offline by focusing on high-calibre customer service and building emotional connections with consumers. Similarly, the customer experience is defining the luxury winners in digital. And creating meaningful, unique and memorable experiences can only be achieved through extensive testing and feedback.

As I mentioned earlier in this book, businesses that adopt agile approaches to project management will increase their chances of success. Digital marketing and the skills required will continue to evolve and change at an accelerated rate. The digital winners will be those who commit to lifelong learning.

DIGITAL SPARKLE

In digital, you need to have a tight feedback loop so that you can quickly optimise your strategies. For luxury brands in particular, taking into account customer feedback is crucial, as is incorporating emerging requirements, new learnings and innovative ideas to the process.

In an ever-changing environment driven by digital technologies, the linear traditional marketing strategy process is no longer effective. Instead, smart marketers know they need to stay nimble and implement responsive campaigns and strategies in iterative loops, where decisions are guided by data and continual testing. Here's what to focus on:

- *Customer insights:* listen to your customers to craft digital assets that address precise audience motivations and needs. Harness customer feedback, measure progress and make real-time adjustments to improve outcomes.

- *Integrated team collaboration:* clarify any changes necessary for successful execution and keep all key stakeholders in sync in terms of the goals and agenda.
- *Real-time responsiveness:* pay attention to current cultural phenomena and relevant events in real time to capitalise on spotlight opportunities. Consider Oreo's quick-thinking response to the power outage during the Super Bowl a few years back, for example. They tweeted an ad that read 'You can still dunk in the dark' that went viral. This was a smart way to direct an existing buzz of attention to their own brand.

PAUSE AND PONDER

- How often do you assess your digital performance, and how do you use this assessment to make changes?

- Do you listen to feedback from your customers and respond quickly to feedback and current trends?

CHAPTER 12

Working With an Agency

I TALK to premium and luxury businesses every day, both large and small. I've observed that even though luxury marketers and business owners have a deep knowledge of their particular industry, they often feel overwhelmed by digital and what it means specifically for their particular business. Many of the brands I come across don't have a proper digital marketing plan, don't have the resources, or don't have a clear understanding of how digital can help grow their bottom line.

Some of the biggest barriers I see preventing luxury brands from engaging in digital marketing and social media activity are:

- lack of buy-in from top of organisation
- lack of resources
- lack of knowledge or understanding

- unsupportive company culture
- fear of reputation issues
- conflict of interest between different departments
- perceptions of industry regulation
- inability to measure success
- insufficient skill level within external agency
- lack of budget
- disagreement over ownership or lack of ownership
- lack of awareness about opportunities

Among the typical areas of concern are:

- whether or not to work with a digital agency
- what level of resources should be allocated to digital
- what skills and knowledge are required
- what is the value of digital for both brands and customers

So let's explore all these concerns and sometimes misconceptions.

This chapter is all about giving you the right mindset to ask the right questions, whether they are addressed to yourself and your business, external parties or your customers.

Why Work with a Digital Agency?

I hear several common beliefs and perplexities relating to working with external agencies all the time.

These are:

- Working with external agencies is expensive.
- I think it's better and more cost-effective to manage a digital team in-house.
- I don't know what I should outsource.
- I don't trust agencies.
- I don't understand what exactly agencies are doing and what I pay for.

I also hear every day stories of people who had bad experiences with agencies and, as a result, assumed that digital was not performing and thus no longer worth investing in. And that's a reality I have also experienced firsthand in the course of my career when marketing on the client side. When working in the marketing department in-house, I too have met with several agencies, been lied to countless times and promised things that were not followed through on, and become frustrated by the lack of transparency and the confusing use of jargon. The results were misalignment and missed opportunities.

I now realise not all agencies are created equal—some are good and some are not so good (terrible, even). In order to work successfully with an agency, you should look at this relationship between agency and client as a partnership built on trust and respect. The digital agency should be seen as an extension of your team. And remember, digital success requires practise and perseverance.

Developing a Hybrid System

The scenario when considering working with an agency used to be very straightforward. Your company either had the internal skills to manage digital marketing in-house or needed to hire an external agency. Today, with the rise and spread of digital, we have started to see a hybrid system more and more, whereby businesses seek sophisticated digital marketing support even if they already have an in-house marketing team.

DIGITAL SPARKLE

Given the complexity and ever-evolving nature of digital marketing, in-house marketing departments are now commonly seeking help and partnering with external digital professionals to guide them through the maze and help them master all the nuances, tools, platforms and strategies to effectively leverage digital.

The best clients I have are those who want to learn what my agency is doing and why we are doing it. Engaged clients often means they see value in our work, and want to work with us to manage their digital strategy.

So when working with a digital marketing agency, always consider how you can benefit from knowledge transfer and how empowering the digital agency is. Here are some value-adds you can gain from working with the right digital agency:

- *A digital agency gives you access to a team of experts:* I am always shocked to hear that businesses (even big established brands) still rely on interns or very junior staff to 'oversee' their social media strategies and other digital projects. Sorry to disappoint you, but just because you are young and can use social media platforms doesn't make you good at digital marketing.

- *A digital agency brings you up-to-date information:* what worked today in digital may not work tomorrow. Working with a digital agency often ensures your business follows the best practices and is aware of the latest trends. This helps in-house team members, who often can't keep up with the latest information and trends simply because they need to focus on multiple areas.

- *A digital agency can set realistic benchmarks:* although the definition of digital success differs (and should differ) depending on your brand and business, you still need to know if your digital efforts are working or failing. This can be difficult to measure, especially if you are new at digital and you don't have much historic data to compare your performance to. An experienced digital marketing agency, however, can benchmark your efforts against other 'similar' clients and give you some indication of where you stand.

- *A digital agency has an outside-in view of your business:* when an agency steps in, they will look at your business with a fresh perspective and will thus be able to see things that you might have never noticed on your own. They will help breathe new life into your project and help you plan new ones. Many clients have thrown themselves into digital marketing without even building a strong foundation for their future success.
- *A digital agency helps you maintain digital momentum:* one of the most common pitfalls for businesses is that they launch a digital project but then fail to quickly see the initial outcomes they were expecting. This often means the project rapidly loses momentum or stakeholders quickly get discouraged and give up too early. But to achieve true success you need to nurture your audience(s)—which can take time—and know when to adapt or change rather than abandon. Working with an agency can help with defining strategies for the long haul.

Choosing the Right Digital Partner

A lot of time and planning can go into getting all the approvals required from internal stakeholders and budgeting completed for a new project, so it is important that you choose from the very start the digital partner that will work best with your company. Further, the types of services and the level of service that are offered can vary greatly from one agency to another and, with so many digital agencies to choose from, choosing the right digital agency can be a daunting prospect. I know that the various offerings can sound hugely complex and expensive if you do not understand the true value digital will bring to your business. For small businesses in particular, there's often a gap between what they need and what they can afford. So before you jump into a long-term contract, you need to properly assess your options—and if you feel overwhelmed by the promises made by different agencies, read on.

Because I run a creative and digital marketing agency that works with premium and luxury brands, I've gained a great deal of insight into what works and doesn't work in terms of client–agency dynamics. So when it comes to finding the right digital agency to partner with, here are the pointers that can help you identify the right match for you:

- *No jargon:* refrain from using agencies that try to baffle you with digital jargon. A great agency won't try to impress you with fancy technicalities. Instead, they will make sure you understand what benefits they can specifically bring to your business and let their results do the talking.
- *Transparency:* this is an area where many digital agencies fall short. Yet transparency is essential if you want to have a true partner in the success of your business. When selecting your digital agency, make sure to choose one that you feel

comfortable to talk to, ask questions of, and have an open dialogue with about the project.

- *Diligence and agility:* you should always work with an agency that is structured and diligent. Turn to agencies with demonstrated track records of success, starting with their own brand. Marketers know how to talk the talk. But can the agency walk the walk? Make sure your digital agency is planning to set some KPIs and include some level of reporting measures in their process, so that you can easily and effectively calculate ROI. You need to know what kind of results you can expect, rather than be left wondering, month after month, whether the agency is producing results. It's crucial for you and the agency to define objectives and evaluation criteria before inking a deal. Also check whether the agency has people with the right experience and a proven and tested methodology. Your digital agency should spend time understanding your business and be able to regularly articulate your ultimate goals and align them with time-framed deliverables. Processes are vital, but inflexible strategies are recipes for disaster. A good agency knows when to evaluate, refine and reiterate.
- *Bespoke:* work with an agency that will customise their approach to your needs—not just roll out some sort of 'one-size-fits-all' approach. You should refrain from using service packages, because true value comes from bespoke strategies. Also consider whether people at the agency are good listeners.

You need to invest in an agency that invests its heart in your business and helps you build sustainable growth, based on what you have discussed. All services should be specifically designed for you, according to your specific set of requirements.

- *Chemistry:* find partners, not just providers or vendors. At the end of the day, you do business with people, so make sure you choose an agency you feel comfortable with, where the right people are in place to get you to where you need to be. An agency is often considered an extension of your brand team. How do you feel about the people you've met with? How aligned are you on values, culture, communication styles, outlook and personality?

- *Empowerment:* remember the old saying 'sharing is caring'? Refrain from opting for agencies that are very mysterious. One of my clients, a premium furniture company, said to me that what made them choose us over other agencies was that we were the only digital agency they had met that had actually come to the introductory meeting and shared some specific areas of improvement the business could implement, with or without our help.

- *Collaboration:* business owners tend to underestimate the level of involvement they should provide. But working with a digital marketing agency should be a collaborative relationship. The right agency looks to creatively provide you with the best possible results for your business, so you want an agency that can enhance your understanding of how to attract and engage your audience. If an agency is not asking questions about your business, they're probably not worth the time. You want an agency that works closely with you. You should, of course, ask questions and give your own insights, but you also need to be open to opinions and recommendations—and a good agency should provide these.

- *Creativity:* for luxury brands, creative visuals and aesthetics play a critical role in maintaining the allure and status of the brand online. Working with an agency that has impeccable taste can make a difference. You want to make sure that everything developed for you will be crafted to perfection.
- *Integrated strategy:* you cannot build digital marketing strategies and campaigns in silos. Your digital strategies must be fully integrated with your traditional activities, and working with an agency that understands marketing and its overall ecosystem can make a difference. You want to choose an agency that includes more than pure technicians—one that can also provide strategic guidance.

Working Out How Much to Spend on Digital Marketing

Perhaps you've heard the saying, 'The bitterness of poor quality remains long after the sweetness of low price is forgotten.' Even though the original author of this quote is unclear (some sources attribute it to Benjamin Franklin), it has always resonated with me.

When meeting a client for the first time, the question of the budget naturally always pops out. And because digital is a new ecosystem, many clients feel unsure about how much such services should cost. A further impact is that digital is, unfortunately, still often considered a side activity, meaning business owners and marketers tend to compare vendors solely based on prices. This all means a lot of business owners make the mistake of just looking at the final price without looking deeper. By opting for the cheapest option, however, you are overlooking the most important criteria: quality.

Countless times I have seen thousands of dollars wasted and frustration built-up due to poor and quick decisions. Don't get me wrong: the highest price does not always mean the highest quality. You will need to assess the agency's ability to meet *your* business requirements. But do keep in mind that quality and results take precedence over the enticement of low prices. Digital opens avenues to amazing opportunities for innovative luxury brands—including deeper engagement with con-sumers, increased efficiency, sustainable growth and reduced costs in the long run. Your focus should be on how much value (in the sense of worthy and valuable long-term results) an agency's strategy provides, and the benefits your brand can get out of it.

So now you must be thinking… *okay, but how much should I invest in digital?*

The answer to this question, however, is rather complex and will depend on a variety of criteria, such as your business size, your industry, your competitors, your level of digital readability, your in-house capabilities, how much you want to grow your business—and the list goes on and on. Prices also vary drastically from one agency to another, and depending on the scope of the project. So instead of focusing purely on the price you need to pay, look at the returns you can get, and think about how much you should be allocating to digital as a proportion of your total marketing budget.

Is it always more expensive to work with an external agency rather than developing an internal team? Not necessarily. Let's think about it for a minute. Digital can mean various things depending on the stage of your business and its specificities. As a bare minimum, you will most likely need someone to optimise your website (a web developer), someone to optimise your rankings in search results (SEO specialist), someone to publish quality content regularly (content manager) and someone to engage with your audience in social media (community manager). This scenario would mean that you would need to recruit a minimum of four employees to handle your digital marketing activities. And depending on your budget, you might only be able to afford entry-level staff with no prior experience in the field. Also, recruiting internal digital staff does not necessarily mean you will not need to work with an external agency.

If an agency does not take the time to listen and ask questions about your business, you will most likely not see the true value of digital for your business.

DIGITAL SPARKLE

One thing is certain. If you do decide to work with an agency, you should always choose a digital partner that takes the time to understand your business and provide you with bespoke services, because not all businesses require the same digital solutions.

People also often ask me if it is better to work with a one-stop agency or multiple specialised agencies. Once again, it depends. But if you opt for multiple agencies, you must make sure they can effectively communicate with each other. If not, you will end up with a digital cacophony of fragmented, inconsistent and sometimes incompatible strategies. As explained earlier in this book, it is important that your digital implementation is well integrated to offer seamless results across all your touchpoints.

Another aspect you may be considering is where you should be investing your digital spend—that is, which channels to focus on?

Indeed, when talking to luxury professionals, I have noticed that too often they invest money in the wrong channels. This is where you have scenarios whereby marketers invest in channel A while the majority of their customers spend most of their time online on channel B. So the answer to this problem is both tricky and simple. You need to invest where your customers are.

When discussing digital strategy with brand marketers and business owners, I am often surprised to hear that they invest a lot less in digital than other marketing mediums. In fact, many businesses allocate less than 10 per cent of their marketing budget to digital. Business owners have to change the way they look at digital and the implications it has on the overall business and bottom line. As the importance of a strong digital presence is becoming more important for businesses, extra attention should be given to the place of digital in your overall business ecosystem and you should invest in digital accordingly.

While I can't give you clear benchmarks for how much you should invest in digital, you should definitely make sure that you are investing smart and future-proofing your business. As I mentioned in chapter 9, for example, some luxury brands such as Burberry have taken such a fully integrated approach to digital that they allow over 60 per cent of their marketing budget for digital.

Another point I would like to add relates to the discussions of budget between client and agency. Because many clients exclusively focus on trying to get the cheapest possible price, they approach various agencies without sharing their budget upfront—an approach that can be time-consuming for both the client and the agency. If you are not transparent with the agency, chances are the proposal you get back will be completely misaligned with your available resources and the scope of the project. By telling the agency your allocated budget, you will avoid rounds and rounds of amended proposals or, worse, the agency dropping out after you have spent days or months discussing the project because you simply do not meet their minimum range.

Knowing What the Problem Is (That's the Problem)

Another quote commonly attributed to Albert Einstein is, 'If I had an hour to solve a problem, I'd spend 55 minutes thinking about the problem and 5 minutes thinking about solutions.' (Again, doubt exists as to whether Einstein ever said this.) Even though the source is unclear, and even though I personally don't think it outlines the perfect proportion, this quote nevertheless illustrates an important point: before trying to solve a problem, you should spend time understanding and clearly defining what the problem really is.

Unfortunately, what I have observed when tackling digital projects is that businesses fail to realise that the quality of the solutions will greatly depend on how well they have defined the problems their customers want them to solve.

People often say, 'The first step to recovery is recognising you have a problem', right? I agree. And I am seeing a lot of businesses recognising they have a problem with digital.

However, when many businesses notice a problem, they look for a solution that can make the symptoms disappear... quickly! They often look for bandages instead of treating the actual source of the problem. You need to spend time and resources on investigating the roots of the problem, and making sure you are working on the right problem. You need to understand the struggles and goals of your consumers.

I often hear stories of people approaching agencies and telling them, for example, that their problem is they need to build an app or an e-commerce site. But these are not problems; these are potential solutions. Before you even consider rushing into a new digital project, you need to ask yourself what it is that you are trying to solve for your users. What's their problem? Be curious. Ask questions and gather facts.

Investigate the causes and circumstances of the problem. Let's assume, for example, that the problem stated by your customer is, 'I hate shopping for your luxury products online'. The solution to this problem might not be obvious. However, if you dig deeper and realise the real problem is, 'I get lost in your website navigation during checkout', the stumbling blocks and the solutions are clearer. You know that you need to simplify your shopping cart process. Of course, you'll still need to work on the implementation, but the steps to this solution become clearer.

Without the essential step of fully understanding the problem, you will most likely waste money and resources, and end up pursuing digital initiatives that aren't aligned with what your consumers need and want.

Now think about it. Should you wait to get in terrible pain before you try to make it go away? Or is it more effective to be proactive and ensure your business remains healthy? What do you think will be most effective and efficient?

I invite you to take some time to identify and really understand the fundamental issues that your business is facing, keeping in mind that an agency can also be a valuable source of helping you understand your brand's challenges.

PAUSE AND PONDER

- Have you worked with agencies in the past? If so, what were some of the positives of the experience? What were the negatives?

- Do you see some gaps in your in-house experience where an agency could help?

- Have you allocated enough to your digital spend (whether you're working with an agency or not)?

- Do you need some help truly understanding where the problems lie with your digital strategy and your customers' online experience? Could an agency help with this?

Final Thoughts

LUXURY marketers' fear of losing control of their brands, coupled with a lack of digital and social media skills, has contributed to the late adoption of digital by the luxury sector. And old habits die hard, especially when luxury brands have been so successful for so long with traditional marketing. But the whole field of marketing is changing— and luxury marketing is no exception. Digital is redefining customer experiences and consumer engagement, and luxury marketers today can no longer ignore it.

Luxury consumers are highly digital and their expectations are continually rising, so the question is no longer whether or not luxury brands should embrace digital, but how they should go about doing it.

There is no one way to developing a digital strategy for your luxury brand, but rather many possible routes to successfully leverage digital. But what's important is that you do it consistently and with a specific strategic intent. I hope that this book has further inspired you to grow stronger.

Marketers at all levels are struggling to keep up with the fast-paced nature of the industry and to adapt to rapidly changing customers.

With so many digital media available, marketers need to prioritise their initiatives around driving value for consumers, in order to stay relevant. New technologies, mobile access and the social web have all brought a new level of complexity to marketing departments and overall business organisations. And luxury brands are playing catch up.

More data are available than ever before. Luxury marketers need to learn to make sense of the data and develop insights that help improve the value they bring to customers.

Having worked with premium and luxury brands for years, I've learnt what makes digital so powerful and how it is shaping the future of the luxury sector. To thrive in these changing times, luxury businesses must understand the new needs of consumers and how to adapt effectively to these. Luxury marketers do need to make a real effort to learn essential skills, such as digital marketing, analytics and broader technology skills. Learning these new skills does not mean that their previous wealth of knowledge is no longer valid. But those principles need to be adapted to new requirements.

Marketing for the digital age is a long journey and will continue to evolve, enabled by the continuous developments of technology. You will need to look after many aspects along the way—from ensuring you maintain your luxury brand values to fully engaging and constantly learning from your customers. Things may move too fast and sometimes you may get frustrated because you do not see the results fast enough. However, you simply can't grow a sustainable luxury business without embracing digital.

Chasing Quick Fixes versus Long-Term Vision

By its very nature digital encourages a prizing of immediacy. Everything is live—real-time, always on. Right here, right now. But the biggest mistake I see businesses make is to look at digital projects as quick-fixes. Instead, businesses must think beyond this immediacy and look at how digital can help them achieve their long-term vision and achieve significant and sustainable growth.

Of course, we all want people to immediately respond to our communications and you should be monitoring this responsively. But, ultimately, what matters most is long-term brand engagement, and so you should look at digital as a long-term strategy for your business. Digital is not a quick fix, it's a journey (and an exhilarating one at that).

Don't make the same mistake and look for temporary and quick solutions when leveraging digital for your brand. Instead, aim to make a permanent mindset change and truly adapt to the new challenges. At the end of the day, what's more important for your luxury brand is creating the fertile ground for a fruitful long relationship with your audience.

Digitally Forward

Getting digital right and reinventing the relationships and experiences for the digital age should be a priority across the luxury industry—and, in particular, among luxury SMEs and niche brands. Digital is most importantly a great opportunity to deeply connect and engage with your customers, and luxury brands should use digital to continue to focus on this fundamental need. This means fully integrating all your existing and potential channels, and offering luxury shoppers a seamless experience across all of them.

Luxury marketers must work to see how they can apply their essence and promise across digital platforms, so they can be more nimble in the future. Remember that the digital transformation journey is both complex and rewarding. It requires very targeted, informed and integrated efforts that recognise the nuances and allure of the luxury sector and answer the higher expectations of the affluent consumers. The choice is yours: embrace digital or risk being left out.

Through this book, I have shared some traits to help you *Shine* in the digital age. Attempt to adopt them as your own. Plan and have a clear vision (Strategy), adopt an integrated approach when executing your plan (Holistic implementation), interpret data to make informed decisions (Intelligence), stay agile and be ready to react and adapt quickly (Nimbleness) and last but definitely not least, connect with your audience and engage in conversations (Engagement).

I hope that the framework and insights shared in this book have given you some food for thought that will be helpful in your own business journey, helping you avoid costly mistakes and develop well-thought-out digital strategies.

Next Steps

The finish line for digital marketing does not exist. Instead, winning means continuously crossing into the next tier of success, leading your company to sustainable growth. My main aim with this book is to not only make you think and question your current strategies but also empower you to perform on a whole new level. You have read this book for a reason and that reason is to take action. With that in mind, I invite you to share your experience with other readers on this book's companion site. It's a great platform to interact with me and the broader luxury community, and you'll also find links to further reading, materials and resources that I think are valuable. I also invite you to follow me on my various social media channels to be kept informed on the latest trends in marketing for luxury brands.

shinedigitalluxury.com

Remember: digital is here to stay and the promises it holds for luxury brands are bright. I certainly believe so, based on my experience and doing what we can to grow luxury businesses, particularly with luxury SMEs in Asia and around the world.

More than this book's content, it is the mindset shift that it advocates that is most important. So you may decide to read this book again, to really make the shift to seeing the power of digital. The steps that will then follow are the ones that matter most: how you 'make it happen' and take your first steps towards becoming a modern luxury brand.

29122356R00131

Made in the USA
San Bernardino, CA
11 March 2019